# FACILITATOR GUIDE

LEGACY
Leadership
INSTITUTE

ISBN: 978-0-9974943-0-3

**THE LEGACY LEADERSHIP® FACILITATOR'S GUIDE.** Copyright 2002, Revised 2007/2016. CoachWorks® International, Inc., Dallas, Texas USA. All rights reserved. The Legacy Leadership® Model, Program and System was written and developed by Dr. Lee Smith and Dr. Jeannine Sandstrom. No part of this publication may be reproduced in any form, or by any means whatsoever without written permission from the publisher, except in the case of brief quotations embodied in critical articles and reviews with appropriate acknowledgements.

CoachWorks®, Legacy Leader®, Legacy Leaders®, Legacy Leadership®, The Legacy Leadership® Institute™, The Legacy Leadership® 5 Best Practices™, Legacy Leadership® Model™, The Legacy Leadership® Competency Inventory (LLCI)™, LegacyShifts™, The Legacy Counsel (TLC)™, The Legacy Forum™, Legacy Leader® Coach™, Executive Workout™, Collaborative Conversation™, Holder of Vision and Values™, Creator of Collaboration and Innovation™, Influencer of Inspiration and Leadership™, Advocator of Differences and Community™, Calibrator of Responsibility and Accountability™, Executive Workout Track™, and RealTime Legacy™.

CoachWorks® Press, Dallas, TX USA.

**CoachWorks® International Corporation**
*The Legacy Leader Company®*
Dallas, Texas USA

www.CoachWorks.com
www.LegacyLeadership.com
info@coachworks.com

# Welcome Facilitators!

## Welcome to Legacy Leadership® Facilitation
We are very happy that you have chosen to join us in distributing Legacy Leadership® learning. **Our mission is to have a Legacy Leader® in every organization around the world.** By joining us through use of this Facilitator Guide, you will be able to use and pass along to others a model of leadership that works in the best of times and the worst of times. It is a model with enduring qualities that immediately applies to many businesses as well as life issues. It also adds to and maximizes what is working well in an organization.

## CoachWorks® Dedication
CoachWorks® is dedicated to providing high quality product and enduring support. We also are dedicated to having leaders learn through the use of the best type of adult learning: facilitative process versus lecture. We want you to model a real live "leader at work" environment in the Institute in order for participants to leave with the idea that Legacy Leadership® applies to the way they live, as opposed to merely being a good thing to use on occasion. We are also dedicated to having every leader shift to thinking about how they pass on the learning to others; Legacy Leaders® intentionally develop others.

## What We Want For You
Now that you have been through the Institute yourself, you can see the depth of this model. What we want most for you is:

- To become a student of leadership yourself—to immerse yourself in Legacy Leadership®.

- To be intentional about your own development so you walk your talk.

- To accumulate stories from your own business experiences that immediately apply to telling the story of how Legacy Leadership works.

- To become a master facilitator for life as you facilitate Legacy Leadership®.


So, we welcome you on board. We will be available, with the help of our Master Facilitators, for your extended learning. Our focus is on having each of you be your best, as you do the same for others.


*Lee and Jeannine*

The LEGACY Leader Company

# Table of Contents

WELCOME ............................................................................................................................................ 3
Introductory Notes ............................................................................................................................. 5
Institute Big Picture ............................................................................................................................ 8

**DAY 1** ................................................................................................................................................. 9
**Overview** ......................................................................................................................................... 10
    Preparation ................................................................................................................................. 12
    Target Goals ............................................................................................................................... 13
  **Morning**
    Session 1-1: Welcome and Introductions ............................................................................ 15
    Session 1-2: Institute Overview ............................................................................................. 16
    Session 1-3: Legacy Leadership and General Leadership Overview/Discussion .......... 18
  **Afternoon**
    Session 1-4: Competencies and Legacy .............................................................................. 23
    Session 1-5: Reflection/Wrap/Calibration ........................................................................... 26
  **Facilitator's Personal Notes, Day 1** ......................................................................................... 27

**DAY 2** ............................................................................................................................................... 28
**Overview** ......................................................................................................................................... 29
    Preparation ................................................................................................................................. 33
    Target Goals ............................................................................................................................... 34
  **Morning**
    Session 2-1: Welcome/Teachback/Homework Debrief/LL-BP Review ........................... 36
    Session 2-2: Best Practice #1 .................................................................................................. 37
    Session 2-3: Best Practice #5 .................................................................................................. 40
    Session 2-4: Bridging the Gap Between BP1 and BP5 ...................................................... 41
  **Afternoon**
    Session 2-5: Best Practice #3 .................................................................................................. 43
    Session 2-6: Situational Story Development (SSD) ............................................................. 45
    Session 2-7: Reflection/Wrap/Calibration ........................................................................... 52
  **Facilitator's Personal Notes, Day 2** ......................................................................................... 53

**DAY 3** ............................................................................................................................................... 54
**Overview** ......................................................................................................................................... 55
    Preparation ................................................................................................................................. 58
    Target Goals ............................................................................................................................... 59
  **Morning Session**
    Session 3-1: Welcome/Teachback/Homework Debrief ..................................................... 61
    Session 3-2: Best Practice #2 .................................................................................................. 62
    Session 3-3: Best Practice #4/PCSI ....................................................................................... 65
  **Afternoon**
    Session 3-4: Analysis and Planning ....................................................................................... 72
    Session 3-5: Summaries ........................................................................................................... 74
    Session 3-6: Reflection/Wrap/Final Calibration/Celebration .......................................... 76
  **Facilitator's Personal Notes, Day 3** ......................................................................................... 77

**RESOURCES: Legacy Leadership® Review Master (Answers)** .............................................. 78

# Introductory Notes

## Design Principles

The Legacy Leadership® Institute is a uniquely-designed program that is very different from a typical "classroom" experience. These are the core design principles that are critical for the Facilitator to internalize and model to ensure a successful experience for all learners:

1. The overriding principle in the design of this program is that we are <u>leaders teaching other leaders</u> how to be Legacy Leaders® (LL). So, this program is not just about learning HOW to be a Legacy Leader®. It is also about how to GROW future leaders. Learners will be experiencing the entire program from the viewpoint of how to grow others, and how to live their legacy today.

2. In partnership with this principle is that the program is to be practical and **applicable immediately**. Legacy Leadership® offers simple solutions to complex and complicated problems. The Institute's emphasis is on business situations and how to apply the concepts of Legacy Leadership®.

3. **Experiential learning is critical.** The design point is **limited lecture** (very important!) and learn by doing (and teaching others how to do). This is not about the "Instructor" imparting wisdom and knowledge but about truly "facilitating" the content from the learners using the resources available. This means learner-centric, not facilitator-centric. Much of the content of Legacy Leadership can also be self-taught. You will find that incredible learning happens as the participants discuss this seemingly simple yet very profound framework of leadership. The Facilitator often merely stands by as the class teaches itself.

4. Adults learn through a balance of active participation *and* quiet reflection. The program is designed with ample time for both. There is strong evidence to suggest that leaders who spend time journaling and reflecting on their actions are even stronger as leaders. Learners will spend time reflecting each day as well as intensive development planning (with peer coaching) to fully internalize all lessons and experiences.

## Content Delivery

Due to the design principles stated above, the role of Facilitator is to enable the <u>process</u> of learning versus the <u>standard transfer of knowledge</u>. It is assumed that the Facilitator has a deep knowledge (and passion for) Legacy Leadership® and the 5 Best Practices. All Legacy Leadership® Institutes are to be delivered/facilitated ONLY by completely trained and certified Level 2 Legacy Leadership® Facilitators. It is assumed and intended that those persons facilitating any LLI will know Legacy Leadership® well, practice it, promote it in their workplaces and be easily able to transfer knowledge of it. This guide is NOT intended to be used by anyone not trained to Legacy Leadership® Level 2 certification requirements.

The major content of Legacy Leadership® is delivered via the exercises, discussions and debriefs throughout the entire Institute using:

- **extensive open-ended questioning techniques** (i.e.: "which BP does that relate to?" or "how has that exercise drawn out the essence of BPX?" or "as a Legacy Leader, how would you handle this type of situation?" or "it sounds like you are talking about a Holder of Vision.... etc.)

- **ability to draw out the experiences** of the learners.

- **intuitive skill** at highlighting one's own and others' stories and linkages to illustrate key learning points.

# Introductory Notes

- **ultimate flexibility with flow** and timing (while honoring learning objectives) to seize powerful learning opportunities.

- **consideration for alternatives** for different styles of learners.

- **linkages from previous modules** and lead-ins to upcoming lessons.

- ability to be comfortable **allowing participants to teach themselves** and arrive at their own "aha's" as material is debriefed.

The Facilitator will use these techniques in concert with the various materials available. We have combined three documents into one convenient resource called the Participant Workbook. Each participant should have one of these workbooks. This book contains the following:

- **The Learning Journal** (All exercises and note-taking sheets for the Institute, Homework Assignments, other Resource materials)
- **The Field Guide** *(Reference Manual)*
- **The LL Model** (printed in color on the back of the Participant workbook))
- **LLCI** (Legacy Leadership Competency Inventory™)

In addition, the Facilitator should use this Facilitator Guide, as well as any optional materials desired (such as Legacy Leadership Playing Cards, PCSI (Personal Coaching Styles Inventory) other resources, AND the expertise of Legacy Leadership in the room.

## About This Facilitator's Guide Book

One of the unique qualities of the Legacy Leadership® Institute is its intentional design for participants to teach themselves the content of the 5 Best Practices, the platform on which Legacy Leadership® stands. This Institute has a "minimal Lecture" policy. Instead, designers have implemented unique opportunities in which the content materials of Legacy Leadership® are essentially "self-taught" through experiential learning. For that reason, this Facilitator's Guide is most likely somewhat different than others you have encountered. Every Facilitator will deliver this Institute in a different way, due especially to the "process delivery" nature of the Institute. It is expected that those who facilitate the Legacy Leadership® Institute will **KNOW the content material backwards and forwards**, and will therefore be able to facilitate naturally from a place of experience and comfort, rather than from a lecture format. This guide is structured so that you as Facilitator have the opportunity and the space to tailor your facilitation personally. Here's what you can expect to find here:

### Legacy Leadership Content

The content material of the 5 Best Practices, and the Institute in general, is found in the Participant Workbook. It is not expected that you will use all the material available there or here in the Facilitator's Guide. It is here for your quick reference and your customization process. We suggest that you thoroughly familiarize yourself with the content material in the Participant Workbook and this Facilitator Guide. It is up to you what material you deliver, and how and when it is delivered. This guide is provided as just that—a guide. While the material and outlines contained here are suggested and we hope you do deliver most of this material, as long as the basics of Legacy Leadership® are presented, the facilitator is free to shape the Institute as desired, and as may be dictated by individual and group dynamics.

# Introductory Notes

### Module Timing
The planned timing of the Institute is built in various modules in each day. For your quick reference, we have included a symbol like the one at the right which indicates the time allotted for each module. While the timing for most of these are somewhat flexible, the clock certainly must be considered. Another symbol, shown here, is used to indicate that the facilitator needs to keep going at this point.

> 11:10 am — 11:40 am
> 30 Minutes

### NOTE ABOUT INSTITUTE TIMING
On Days 1 and 2, the scheduled time for the Institute is 9:00 am to 4:00 pm. The days are scheduled for beginning and completion within this time frame. However, some may wish to begin earlier and/or end later in order to have more time flexibility. This is at Facilitator's choice.

Also note that the end time noted for Day 3 is later, at 4:30 rather than 4:00 pm in order to allow time for end of Institute celebration, certificates, and discussion of continuing opportunities for legacy community.

Facilitator should determine desired start and stop times, then work within the printed time notations to accommodate selected scheduling.

### Facilitator's Notes
Pages are formatted so that you have space for your facilitation or personal notes. You may wish to make note of something you have found in the content material that you want to incorporate at a particular time. Rather than assume all people facilitate in exactly the same way, we have given this customizable option. Occasionally, we have made notes with further instructions to the Facilitator. We have also provided a page for notes at the end of each day's facilitation instructions.

### Big Picture View
Immediately following this introductory material you will find the complete overview of all three days of the Institute.

### Daily Outlines
Tables showing a detailed look at the timing and generalized content of each day's events ("Day Overview") are presented in the front of each day's notes.

### Preparation
For each day a simple listing of materials, equipment and pre-Institute preparations are given immediately after the daily outline. Facilitators should personalize these pages beforehand listing any information they need to adequately prepare in advance for each day's delivery.

### Target Goals
An explanation of the intent and objectives for each module are presented immediately following the Preparation page, and before the beginning of the daily Facilitator notes.

# Institute Big Picture

| Day 1 | Day 2 | Day 3 |
|---|---|---|
| **Session 1:** (Getting Started)<br>- Welcome<br>- Leader/Partner (Time for Developing Relationships) | **Session 1:** (Starting the Day)<br>- Teachbacks<br>- Homework debrief<br>- Quick overview of 5 BPs | **Session 1:** (Starting the Day)<br>- Teachbacks<br>- Homework debrief |
| **Session 2:** (Institute Overview)<br>- Legacy Leadership Institute Overview (Roadmap to set direction) | **Session 2:** (Best Practice 1)<br>- Defining the Terms<br>- Content Delivery<br>- "How To" and "Important Pieces" (Prep) | **Session 2:** (Best Practice 2)<br>- Defining the Terms<br>- Content Delivery<br>- Aerotech Briefing<br>- Trust Assessment |
| **MORNING BREAK** | **MORNING BREAK** | **MORNING BREAK** |
| **Session 3:** (Legacy Leadership and General Leadership Overview)<br>- Becoming a student of leadership<br>- Intro to LL w/brief overview of 5 BPs<br>- Identify the Ideal Leader (Know, Believe, Do)<br>- Distinctions Between Management and Leadership<br>- Observations and Insights, Open Discussion | **Session 2 (cont.)**<br>- "How To" and "Important Pieces" (Delivery)<br>- Debrief<br><br>**Session 3:** (Best Practice 5)<br>- Set Up (the other bookend practice)<br>- Defining the Terms<br>- Content Delivery Exercise (they teach us)<br><br>**Session 4:** (Bridging the Gap 1 to 5)<br>- Bridging the Gap between BP1-BP5<br>- Observations and Insights, Open Discussion | **Session 3:** (Best Practice 4)<br>- Defining the Terms<br>- Content Delivery<br>- Case Studies (Prep)<br>- Case Studies (Presentations)<br>- PCSI (or other styles tool) |
| **LUNCH** | **LUNCH** | **LUNCH** |
| **Session 4:** (Competencies and Legacy)<br>- LL Playing Cards<br>- Debrief | **Session 5:** (Best Practice 3)<br>- Set-Up<br>- Defining the Terms<br>- Content Delivery<br>- Influential Leader Exercise<br><br>**Session 6:** (Situational Story Development)<br>- Segue and Set-up<br>- Anatomy of a Story<br>- SSD Exercise (Preparation) | **Session 4:** (Analysis and Planning)<br>- LLCI, Part 2, Analysis of Others' LLCI<br>- LLCI, Part 2, Coaching One Another<br>- Development Planning |
| **AFTERNOON BREAK** | **AFTERNOON BREAK** | **AFTERNOON BREAK** |
| **Session 4 (cont.)**<br>- LLCI completion (part 1)<br>- Living Your Legacy (charting their own influence) | **Session 6 (cont.):**<br>- SSD Exercise (Presentations)<br>- Adapting Other Stories (Prep)<br>- Adapting Other Stories (Presentations)<br>- Adapting Other Stories Debrief<br>- Personal Stories with Professional Application<br>- SSD Debrief/Recap | **Session 5:** (Summaries)<br>- Know-Believe-Do Summary<br>- LL Overview-House of Legacy (Prep)<br>- House of Legacy (sharing)<br>- Review Original Objectives |
| **Session 5:** (Completing the Day)<br>- Intro Teachbacks<br>- Personal Reflections<br>- Community Time | **Session 7:** (Completing the Day)<br>- Teachback Set-up<br>- Personal Reflections<br>- Community Time | **Session 6:** (Final Close)<br>- Personal Reflection<br>- Wrap-Up and Community Time<br>- Celebration and Acknowledgement |

# Day 1

# Day 1 – Overview — Morning

| SESSION | CLOCK | TIME ALLOTED | ACTIVITY | DETAILS |
|---|---|---|---|---|
| **1** Welcome and Introductions (9:00—9:40, 40 min) | 9:00-9:10 | 10 minutes | **WELCOME** | Quick welcome to workshop, what it is, etc. including BRIEF intro of what we will be doing today... (go immediately into intro/partners) |
| | 9:10-9:15 | 5 minutes | **LEADER PARTNER INFO** | Explain Leader Partners (for duration of workshop), use introduction sheets in LJ. (participants pair with each other, facilitators pair with each other) |
| | 9:15-9:20 | 5 minutes | **INTERVIEW LEADER PARTNER** | Spend 5 minutes interviewing Leader Partner for introductions (name, business, why attending, expectations, and something fun about person no one would know or suspect) |
| | 9:20-9:35 | 15 minutes | **INTRODUCTIONS** | Partners introduce one another providing information on sheet. |
| | 9:35-9:40 | 5 minutes | **LEADER PARTNER FEEDBACK** | Show pages in Participant Workbook and explain use and purpose of this exercise. Encourage use throughout workshop. Will be shared during individual coaching. |
| **2** | 9:40-10:00 | 20 minutes | **LLI Overview Roadmap to Set Direction** | Overview of institute, daily agendas, objectives, materials (quick review of Participant Workbook). Facilitator(s) to share personal vision for this Institute. This is time to introduce materials, but not content. |
| | 10:00-10:15 | 15 minutes | **BREAK** | Informal, in room or out |
| **3** Leadership, General Overview (10:55—12:00) 1 hr 45 min | 10:15-10:55 | 40 minutes | **INTRODUCTION TO LEGACY LEADERSHIP** | What is it? Review 5 BPs (provide description, Quick Overview) Why is it? (Current business trends, environment, etc.) How did it come to be? (Brief history of CW experience and development of LL) Current application? About becoming a student of leadership. |
| | 10:55-11:25 | 30 minutes | **IDENTIFYING THE IDEAL LEADER** | Use butcher paper, flip chart, etc. to capture thoughts. Ask participants what constitutes the ideal leader (this will be utilized on several occasions later). What does the ideal leader KNOW?<br>What does the ideal leader BELIEVE?<br>What does the ideal leader DO?<br>See what they already know. Key leadership factors. |
| | 11:25-11:45 | 20 minutes | **DISTINCTIONS BETWEEN MANAGEMENT AND LEADERSHIP** | Discuss these important distinctions. Must know before focusing on leadership. Often misunderstood concept about leadership. Discuss/questions. |
| | 11:45-12:00 | 15 minutes | **OBSERVATIONS AND INSIGHTS— Calibration Time** | Spend last few minutes before lunch debriefing what has been discussed. Ask for insights, new observations, personal applications, questions etc. (this time can also be used to have more flexibility for above activities) |
| | 12:00-1:00 | 1 hour | **LUNCH** | In or out (depending on facility) |

*Day 1 continued next page...*

# Day 1 - Overview — Afternoon

| SESSION | CLOCK | TIME ALLOTED | ACTIVITY | DETAILS |
|---|---|---|---|---|
| **4** *Competencies and Legacy (1:00—3:20 - break) 2 hr 5* | 1:00—2:00 | 1 hour | **Legacy Leadership Card Games** | Set cards on every table. Explain any "rules." Let participants play independently, or with facilitation. |
| | 2:00—2:15 | 15 minutes | **Debrief GAME** | Talk about what you saw, realized, learned, why this was informative. |
| | 2:15—2:30 | 15 minutes | **BREAK** | **Informal, in or out** |
| | 2:30—3:00 | 30 minutes | **LLCI, Part 1** | Participants complete LLCI, score, initial questions, set aside for later use. |
| | 3:00—3:20 | 20 minutes | **LIVING YOUR LEGACY (Legacy Charting)** | Explain what this means in regard to Legacy Leadership. Whole purpose is developing other leaders—encourage participants to begin thinking now how they will do that, and with whom. Use either large white board, flip charts, and/or individual sheets to illustrate network effect. Do this in an "org chart" format showing the effects of this kind of leadership. May do in large format and leave in place during Institute, as well as individually on designated sheets in Participant Workbook. |
| **5** *Wrap Time (3:20—4:00) 40 min* | 3:20-3:25 | 5 minutes | **INTRO VOLUNTEER TEACHBACKS** | Explain that each morning a volunteer (or volunteers, partners working together) will be needed to present the previous Day's learnings to the group in 15 minutes time, utilizing any materials they can (Field Guide, charts, etc.) |
| | 3:25-3:35 | 10 minutes | **PERSONAL REFLECTIONS** | Allow participants 10 minutes to write any learnings, reflections on Day 1's activities. Remind about Partner |
| | 3:35—4:00 | 25 minutes | **COMMUNITY TIME (Calibration)** | Time for questions and answers, learning more about each other, questioning of experts, sharing experiences, outstanding learnings, etc. Explain briefly Day 2's more in-depth focus on the BPs. Capture any questions not immediately relevant to the activities at hand earlier in the day, and discuss at this time. |
| | 4:00 | | **CLOSE DAY 1** | **Thank everyone for a great day!** |

## Day 1 SUMMARY

**Morning**

| | | |
|---|---|---|
| Session 1-1 | Welcome and Introductions | 40 minutes |
| Session 1-2 | Institute Overview | 20 minutes |
| *Morning Break* | | |
| Session 1-3 | LL and General Leadership Overview | 1 hour 45 minutes |
| *Lunch* | | |

**Afternoon**

| | | |
|---|---|---|
| Session 1-4 | Competencies and Legacy | 2 hours 20 minutes |
| *Afternoon break in this session* | | |
| Session 1-5 | Wrap/Calibration | 40 minutes |
| *Close* | | |

# Day 1 — PREPARATION

**PREPARATION**

- ☐ All materials available in room:
  - ☐ Participant Material Sets
  - ☐ Flip Charts/Marking Pens (or white boards, etc.)
  - ☐ Pens, pencils, tape, other supplies
  - ☐ Prepare Welcome Flip Chart (or use pre-prepared)
  - ☐ White butcher paper
  - ☐ Other

- ☐ Tables, chairs, etc. set up

- ☐ Legacy Leadership Card Game(s) (afternoon)

- ☐ Butcher paper, or other method (large white board, etc., something that can be preserved during Institute) to capture networking ("Living Your Legacy—Legacy Charting") conversation

# Day 1 — TARGET GOALS

**This day is about becoming a student of leadership.**

### GOALS FOR MORNING SESSION, DAY 1

**Session 1-1: Welcome and Introductions**
- Welcome
- Leader Partner Information
- Interview Leader Partners
- Introduce Leaders
- Leader Partner Feedback

This session is intended to get participants and facilitators familiar with one another, determine personal goals for the Institute (which are to be posted), and introduce the concept of the Leader Partners, including Leader Partner feedback.

**Session 1-2: Institute Overview**
- LLI Overview

The Institute itself is spotlighted by introducing materials and review of agendas and objectives. This provides a roadmap for direction of the Institute.

**Session 1-3: Leadership, General Overview**
- Introduction to Legacy Leadership®
- Identifying the Ideal Leader
- Distinctions Between Management and Leadership
- Observations and Insights

This session is designed to give a broad high-level overview of Legacy Leadership®, from its inception and history to its current applications. The 5 BPs are introduced for the first time here as well. This session's goals are also to highlight the current best thinking of leadership in general, provide insight on the key distinction of leadership vs. management, capture what the participants already know, and establish the path for becoming students of leadership. The observations and insights slot at the end of this time serves several purposes: to debrief what has just been discussed, ask and answer questions, provide personal insights and applications, AND to allow some time flexibility. *(This particular slot has been allocated several times during the Institute for these purposes.)*

*Day 1 Afternoon goals, next page...*

# Day 1 — TARGET GOALS

**GOALS FOR AFTERNOON SESSION, DAY 1**

### Session 1-4: Competencies and Legacy
- Legacy Leadership® Card Game
- Debrief Game
- Legacy Leadership® Competency Inventory™ (LLCI), Part 1
- Living Your Legacy

This session is intended to introduce participants to the fundamental competencies embodied by Legacy Leadership®, primarily through the playing of the game, and the LLCI. The language on the game and the LLCI provides a good overview of concepts embraced by LL. The participants assess themselves with the LLCI and score, but no discussion or interpretation is given at this time other than general discussion. The last part of this session, Living Your Legacy, is intended to help participants understand exactly what Legacy means, and to help them begin planning now to live theirs.

### Session 1-5: Wrap/Calibration
- Intro Volunteer Teachbacks
- Homework Assignment
- Personal Reflections
- Community Time (Calibration time)

Every day of the Institute will end in this manner, requesting volunteers to provide 15-minute teachbacks of the day's content for the following morning (and on this Day 1, actually introducing this concept), assigning homework, allowing time for participants to write their thoughts in the personal Reflections section of the Participant Workbook, and spending the remaining time in conversation with questions and answers regarding the day's content, personal experiences, etc. It is a time to take advantage of the knowledge and experience of the Facilitator(s), and for a general time of sharing. It serves to calibrate the day's events. *(The Community Time at the end of the day is also meant to allow some flexibility in timing of exercises, and to handle discussion of any ideas or questions that cannot be addressed at other times.)*

Facilitator(s) will also remind participants of the Leader Partner Feedback to be completed during their reflection time.

# Day 1 - Morning — Session 1-1

**SESSION 1-1: WELCOME AND INTRODUCTIONS**

🕐 9:00 am—9:40 am
40 Min.

**WELCOME (10 minutes)**

- Welcome
- Leader Partner Info
- Interview Leader Partner
- Introductions
- Leader Partner Feedback Sheets

*(Suggested times shown in parentheses after heading)*

☐ Welcome participants and introduce self, other Facilitator(s) and Guests (if any). Include very BRIEF intro into what you will be doing today.

**LEADER PARTNER INFO (5 minutes)**

☐ Have participants choose a partner. They will have this partner throughout the Institute (determine ahead of time what to do in case of odd number of participants.) Explain that these "partnerships" will be remain throughout the Institute and involved in several exercises.

**LEADER PARTNER INTERVIEW (5 minutes)**

☐ Direct participants to page 14 of the Participant Workbook. Instruct them to spend the next 5 minutes interviewing their partner and obtaining information that will allow them to introduce this person.

**LEADER PARTNER INTRODUCTIONS (15 minutes)**

☐ Allow partners to introduce one another using the information they gathered. Do this as quickly as possible. (15 minutes is allotted.)

☐ As each **personal objective** is read, indicate **how it will be handled** during the Institute: *(for example)*
  - *Yes, it will be covered in the planned agenda.*
  - *This is slightly out-of-scope so let's address it at the end of the day during our calibration time.*
  - *No, this will not be covered – however, there is a lot of expertise here in the room – we encourage you to take best advantage of networking time to get this question answered to your satisfaction. If not by the end of the program, let's be sure we get it answered before you leave.*

☐ **Capture each personal objective** (in bullet point format) on a large chart in room. This chart will remain in sight throughout the Institute and addressed on Day 3.

Legacy Leaderhip® Institute FACILITATOR GUIDE © 2001-2016. COACHWORKS® International. Dallas, TX USA. All Rights Reserved.

# Day 1 - Morning — Session 1-2

**LEADER PARTNER FEEDBACK (5 minutes)**

☐ **Explain concept of Leader Partners.** This program is all about growing leaders. We want to take advantage of the opportunity not only to learn some new skills, but practice them and get feedback on them. So, the person you partnered with is your Leader Partner for the rest of the Institute.

☐ Explain **Leader Partner Feedback** (page 15) In the Participant Workbook. Any time you see a specific leadership behavior that had a positive impact on the group (new idea, something well stated, initiative shown, etc.), take a moment to jot it down on the sheet provided in your journal. Do not share this information yet with your partner. Where possible, indicate which BP(s) this leadership behavior demonstrated. Time will be provided on Day 3 for you to give some quantifiable feedback to your Leader Partner which can be used later in the preparation of a Development Plan. Catch your partner doing something well!

**SESSION 1-2: INSTITUTE OVERVIEW**

**LLI OVERVIEW (20 minutes)**
*This overview serves as a roadmap to set direction for the Institute.*

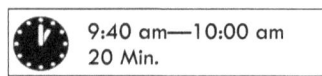
9:40 am—10:00 am
20 Min.

- LLI Overview

*(Suggested times shown in parentheses after heading)*

☐ **Review all materials** available for the Institute.
Answer any questions not previously addressed regarding Institute materials. Walk through the Participant Workbook and briefly explain the layout and contents.

☐ Refer participants to page 16 in the Participant Workbook. Discuss **Institute objectives.**

☐ Discuss the **CoachWorks® vision** of arming participants with enough material, information and inspiration to begin using Legacy Leadership® immediately after (even during!) the Institute.

# Day 1 - Morning — Session 1-2

**SESSION 1-2: INSTITUTE OVERVIEW continued**

☐ **Discuss the Institute Agenda.** (This is suggested agenda for this facilitator guide. Facilitators may slightly alter agendas.)

| DAY 1 | DAY 2 | DAY 3 |
|---|---|---|
| Session 1-1<br>Welcome and Introductions | Session 2-1<br>Welcome/Teachback/Homework Debrief | Session 3-1<br>Welcome/Teachback/Homework Debrief |
| Session 1-2<br>Institute Overview | Session 2-2<br>**Best Practice #1** | Session 3-2<br>**Best Practice #2** |
| Session 1-3<br>Legacy Leadership and General Leadership Overview/Discussion | Session 2-3<br>**Best Practice #5** | Session 3-3<br>**Best Practice #4** |
| | Session 2-4<br>Bridging the Gap Between 1 and 5 | |
| **LUNCH** | **LUNCH** | **LUNCH** |
| Session 1-4<br>Competencies and Legacy | Session 2-5<br>**Best Practice #3** | Session 3-4<br>Analysis and Planning |
| | Session 2-6<br>Storytelling | Session 3-5<br>Summaries |
| Session 1-5<br>Reflection/Wrap/Calibration | Session 2-7<br>Reflection/Wrap/Calibration | Session 3-6<br>Reflection/Wrap/Final Calibration |

☐ **Answer any questions** that might arise about the LLI overview, agenda, etc.

☐ Discuss the **Institute Environment**
*Respect for ALL of us:*
- No cell phones, iPods, PDAs, pagers etc.
- Be here and present
- Respect start/stop times
- No side conversations
- What's said here, stays here

*Respect for EACH of us:*
- All ideas are worthwhile
- We actively grow other Leaders
- We model Best Practices

*General:* (Discuss briefly the logistics of the following:)
- Breaks
- Lunches
- Restrooms
- Phones
- Emergencies
- Messages

# Day 1 - Morning — Session 1-3

**MORNING BREAK (15 minutes)**

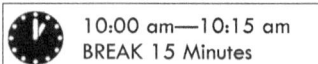
10:00 am—10:15 am
BREAK 15 Minutes

**SESSION 1-3: LEGACY LEADERSHIP® AND GENERAL LEADERSHIP OVERVIEWS**

10:15 am—12:00 pm
1 Hr. 45 Minutes

**INTRODUCTION TO LEGACY LEADERSHIP® (40 minutes)**

- Introduction to Legacy Leadership®
- Identifying the Ideal Leader
- Distinctions Between Management and Leadership
- Observations and Insights (Calibration Time)

*This session draws on the experience, training and knowledge of the Facilitators. This guide does not intend to layout a word-for-word script. Only the highlights are suggested. The Facilitator(s) will fill in "the gaps." This is intended to be informal, conversational, not scripted. The following should be discussed:*

*(Suggested times shown in parentheses after heading)*

☐ **Begin discussion by asking** participants to provide answers to two questions:
- What keeps leaders up at night?
- How has leadership changed in your view?

Allow participants 5 minutes to discuss these questions at their tables, and be ready to present answers as a group.
*(This is optional—see suggestions next page.)*

☐ **Debrief** answers, discuss, and lead into:

☐ **Why Legacy Leadership®, and Why Now?** Discuss current business trends, environment, etc. Direct participants to pages 144-147 of the Participant Workbook. Explain how Legacy Leadership® is a response to these needs.

☐ Facilitate an **informal discussion** about participants' experiences and why there is a need for this type of people/others-oriented model.

*More information and suggestions for this session are on the following pages.* **Review this information prior to presentation.** *Tailor to your delivery style, background and audience.*

**SESSION 1-3: LEGACY LEADERSHIP® AND GENERAL LEADERSHIP OVERVIEW**
continued

**INTRODUCTION TO LEGACY LEADERSHIP continued**

☐ **How did Legacy Leadership® come to be?** Give brief history of this leadership development program. Include background and experiences of program's authors (Drs. Smith and Sandstrom) and Facilitator's background and training in Legacy Leadership® and their passion for this program.

☐ **What is Legacy Leadership®?** (Provide a description using The Model, any other materials Facilitator determines appropriate.) Introduce participants to Participant Workbook and materials inside (only for purposes of this introduction—more detailed look can be made in second part of this section during the LLI Overview.) **Introduce 5 BPs quickly as framework of balanced and comprehensive program.**

☐ **Walk participants through the layout format** of the Field Guide at this time. Explain the "facing page" concept in the layout, and how the two components of each Best Practice are listed on opposite pages—i.e., Vision on the left, Values on the right, etc.):
- **Basic Definitions**
- **Legacy Leadership® Definitions (What it IS, What it is NOT)**
- **Critical Factors (Success and Challenges)**
- **Application (Behaviors and Competencies)**
- **Legacy Steps**
- **Language**
- **LegacyShifts (FROM—TO)**
- **Critical Success Skills**
- **The Aerial View**

☐ **What are current examples of Legacy Leadership® application?** Discuss use in organizations and with individual coaching.

# Day 1 - Morning — Session 1-3

*(IDEAS FOR FACILITATOR PREPARATION: This material is provided as a starting place only for facilitators to develop their own introduction to Legacy Leadership.)*

**Facilitator:** Read all this material carefully beforehand and select your delivery points and methods before the Institute.

**SUGGESTED SET-UP QUESTIONS for discussion:**
1. What keeps leaders up at night?
2. How has leadership changed? (encourage examples)
3. What are books and articles saying?
4. What is the status of, or current trends in leadership today?

**SOME THOUGHTS:**
- To understand Legacy Leadership®, you must become a "student of leadership."
- Leaders are learners/educators.
- Current leader books/articles cover various aspects and techniques of leadership, but do not deliver a comprehensive model.
- Leadership is about character, not position.

**WHAT IS LEGACY LEADERSHIP?**
- A comprehensive framework of practices, behaviors, attitudes and values that addresses every aspect of successful leadership
- A set of 5 Best Practices that changes the culture of an organization from a command post to a community, balanced in its approach to both people and production
- A unique approach to leadership that maximizes professional (personal) and organizational (company) effectiveness
- A philosophy (not a "prescription" plan) of leadership that encourages confidence, learning, wisdom, courage, insight and compassion
- An ageless way to develop personal potential that models real leadership for others
- A highly adaptable model based on developing leaders at all levels
- Each Best Practice has a thought-stopping title (use model)
- The Best Practices focus first on who you BE (i.e., HOLDER), and then on what you DO (i.e., VISION and VALUES)

# Day 1 - Morning — Session 1-3

**SESSION 1-3: LEGACY LEADERSHIP® AND GENERAL LEADERSHIP OVERVIEWS (continued)**

**WHY LEGACY LEADERSHIP® AND WHY NOW?**
- Need for comprehensive model against which to coach individuals either personally (professionally) or within organizations
- Companies have lists of competencies but no model to follow
- Discover what good leaders do, and what business needs them to do
- Trends in leadership

**BACKGROUND OF LEGACY LEADERSHIP®**
- Result of over 40 years combined experience of CoachWorks® principals, Drs. Lee Smith and Jeannine Sandstrom, executive coaches who have always been in the business of developing leaders.
- Have isolated, defined, and made transferable the practices common to leaders who are able to achieve and sustain success with people, product, and revenue.
- Used in year-long emerging leader programs within organizations
- Used for offsites
- LLCI used in all levels of coaching
- Leaders use it for personal development, and for developing others
- Organizations use it for a company-wide leadership model

**NOTES:**
- Be sure to **adequately cover the basic framework of Legacy Leadership® in overview fashion**, carefully introducing with brief descriptions, each of the 5 Best Practices. Use the model, Field Guide, or whatever you wish, but make sure the overall concepts are presented here. The best practices will be covered in depth later, but be sure participants understand overall framework.

- It is very important to bring **current examples of Legacy Leadership®** to light. Facilitator should be prepared to do this, and to ask participants to suggest examples. Participants will want strong evidence of the application of Legacy Leadership® to actual business examples.

## Day 1 - Morning — Session 1-3

**SESSION 1-3: LEGACY LEADERSHIP® AND GENERAL LEADERSHIP OVERVIEWS**
continued

### IDENTIFYING THE IDEAL LEADER (30 minutes)

☐ Begin this segment by **telling a story about an ideal leader** you know. Segue to the question: **what do ideal leaders know, believe and do?** Direct participants to page 17 in the Participant Workbook.

☐ Using butcher paper, or other method to make a large chart, draw lines down the chart to create 3 columns. Label the top of the chart: **"What does the ideal leader…"** Then label each column from left to right KNOW, BELIEVE, and DO. *(You may wish to have this chart made ahead of time, or merely use a chalk or white board available.)*

*Facilitator Note: Please refer to the Participant Workbook page 83. You will find the key page for the KNOW, BELIEVE, DO exercise which is begun here. Please note that your chart will be expanded during the Institute, and will then be debriefed using this information. You will want to have fore-knowledge of this information prior to beginning this exercise. Do NOT refer participants to this page at this time. This is for your information only at this point.*

☐ Facilitate an **informal discussion** about identifying the "ideal leader." Ask participants to offer suggestions to fill in the columns. Have them **think of a leader who has impacted their lives.** What does an ideal leader KNOW? What does an ideal leader BELIEVE? What does an ideal leader DO? Take suggestions and write them in bullet points on the chart. Make sure the chart is big enough to add points to it later, if necessary. This chart will be used throughout the Institute.

☐ While the facilitator is writing on chart, have participants write these ideas in their Participant Workbooks. Explain that we will be coming back to this a number of times.

☐ **OPTION:**
Another option that can be used here is to have one chart for each table group. Ask the groups to discuss the KNOW, BELIEVE and DO chart, trying to limit to top 5 in each category. Have groups report out results and discuss. The purpose of these exercises is for the participants to make their own discoveries about what the LL Model is all about.

### DISTINCTIONS BETWEEN MANAGEMENT AND LEADERSHIP (20 minutes)

☐ Begin by explaining that an important clarification must be made and underscored before proceeding deeper into an understanding of leadership in general, and specifically Legacy Leadership. **Refer participants to pages 157-158 of the Participant Workbook.** The purpose of this general overview is to help them become a "student of leadership," and to begin to guide them in the **study of leaders and leadership.**

# Day 1 - Afternoon — Session 1-3, 1-4

**SESSION 1-3: LEGACY LEADERSHIP® AND GENERAL LEADERSHIP OVERVIEWS**
continued

- ☐ **Take participants through** a reading and discussion of the contents of these pages, explaining that we often misunderstand the differences, but that this distinction is vital to understanding leadership.

- ☐ **Facilitate an informal discussion** about the group's experiences with this concept. Provide question and answer time. Use questions designed to help them see the differences for themselves. For example,
  - "Is setting the direction for a group of people a management effort or a leadership effort?"
  - "Is management actually PART of leadership? How so?"

**OBSERVATIONS AND INSIGHTS (10 minutes)**
*(Calibration time)*

- ☐ Use this time immediately before lunch to debrief what has just been discussed, ask and answer questions, provide personal insights and applications, AND to allow some time flexibility if needed.

**LUNCH (1 Hour)**

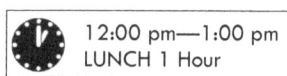
12:00 pm—1:00 pm
LUNCH 1 Hour

**SESSION 1-4: COMPETENCIES AND LEGACY**

1:00 pm—3:20 pm
2 Hours 20 Min.

**LEGACY LEADERSHIP® PLAYING CARDS Game (1 Hour)**

- Legacy Leadership® Playing Cards Games
- Debrief Game
- AFTERNOON BREAK
- LLCI, Part 1
- Living Your Legacy

- ☐ Either play known games or created games whereby participants read and answer the questions on the cards. Play in groups at tables independently. If players do not wish to play a game, merely have them deal cards to each other (i.e., 5 cards each) and one at a time chose one card drawn to answer, one at a time. They may even discuss answers with each other. Facilitator may wish to "invent" a game for play.

*(Suggested times shown in parentheses after heading)*

- ☐ This is a good after-lunch activity that is fun and interactive. You can also allow the participants to create their own games and rules.

# Day 1 - Afternoon — Session 1-4

**SESSION 1-4: COMPETENCIES AND LEGACY continued**

- ☐ Begin play and continue for approximately one hour, or until game(s) reach(es) logical conclusion. Congratulate all players for their honesty and participation. (Facilitators may use this time to play and interact with participants, and/or comment on responses using the dialogue for learning opportunities.)

*Timing Note: This module is intended for 1 HOUR **total** set-up and playing time. Debrief should last 10-15 minutes beyond this. This session can also be shortened or lengthened depending on other activities, at facilitator's discretion.*

**DEBRIEF GAME (10-15 minutes)**

- ☐ Put cards away. Ask questions to debrief this experience.
    - What did this activity reveal to you?
    - What insights were gained about Legacy Leadership®?
    - What did you learn about yourself as a leader?
    - What resources did you draw upon for answers?
    - How did you collaborate?
    - How did you handle conflict, if any?
    - Were there any surprises?
    - How does all this relate to what was learned and shared this morning?

**AFTERNOON BREAK (15 minutes)**

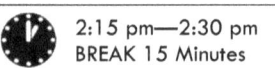
2:15 pm—2:30 pm
BREAK 15 Minutes

**LEGACY LEADERSHIP COMPETENCY INVENTORY (LLCI)**
**Part 1 (30 minutes)**

- ☐ Refer participants to the LLCI. Explain the purpose of the LLCI briefly, and how it will be used later in the Institute. Refer learners to pages 221-223 of the Participant Workbook (LLCI portion) for a simple introduction, and another **VERY brief overview of the 5 BPs**. Explain the LLCI just like you would the first time to a client. Use page 222 to discuss how to complete the LLCI *(You are modeling behavior for the participants!)*

- ☐ Explain that this inventory is used with individuals to help them develop as *Legacy Leaders*.

- ☐ Explain the use of the LLCI, the **10 critical success skills** listed for each Best Practice, etc. NOTE: A collection of skills combine to make a competency (aka: Best Practice)

# Day 1 - Afternoon — Session 1-4

**SESSION 1-4: COMPETENCIES AND LEGACY continued**

**LEGACY LEADERSHIP® COMPETENCY INVENTORY (LLCI) (continued)**

- ☐ Allow participants approximately **20 minutes to complete** the inventory and do their own self-scoring. Remind them this LLCI **exercise will be in two parts.** This is part one only. They will NOT be sharing the results of their assessment at this time. *(NOTE: AFTER participants have completed the LLCI—not before—inform them that they will later share these results with their Leader Partner on Day 3 to both give and receive feedback around the LLCI results.)*

- ☐ **Finish with a few questions** about the LLCI and participants' insights, etc. Part 2 will be on Day 3. (Ask them to put away the LLCIs for now.)

**LIVING YOUR LEGACY (20 minutes)**

- ☐ **Begin by explaining the word LEGACY.** This is the whole purpose of Legacy Leadership®—to develop other leaders. Encourage them to begin thinking right now about who (specifically) they will develop. **This is about Living your Legacy. Legacy is our personal history written and lived in advance.**

- ☐ Discuss the **application of the concepts** they have been discussing all day. Ask them to think with whom they will begin practicing Legacy Leadership, and how.

- ☐ **Ask them "Who will you mentor?"** What other leaders will they begin to develop? Who will they touch? Who do they influence now? Steer their thinking toward a large ever-expanding "organizational chart" format that shows the results of one developing another, developing another, and so on. Ask participants to **capture their own thoughts and draw their own individual charts** on page 19 of the Participant Workbook. Allow some quiet time to do this.

- ☐ At about the half-way point in this exercise, ask participants to move to prepared sheets of paper (large) on walls, posts, or wherever you have room, and use marking pens (this should be set up and prepared in advance) to **write their Legacy Charts** from the notes (first names only) they have just made in their journals. This will remain visible during the remainder of the Institute.

- ☐ After the charts are drawn, stand back and take a look. **Discuss the effects of leaders developing other leaders.** Ask pointed questions to help them understand the driving concept of Legacy Leadership®, as it will apply to their own leadership.
  - Did this exercise surprise them?
  - Does it take the notion of leadership to a new level? How?
  - What legacy will you impart to each person?
  - How will you be intentional in doing this?
  - How will your charts expand?

# Day 1 - Afternoon — Session 1-5

**SESSION 1-5: WRAP/CALIBRATION**

> 3:20 pm—4:00 pm
> 40 Minutes

- Intro Volunteer Teachbacks
- Personal Reflections
- Community Time (Calibration)

### INTRODUCE VOLUNTEER TEACHBACKS (5 minutes)

*(Suggested times shown in parentheses after heading)*

☐ Tell participants that you are looking for volunteers to provide a 10-minute review, or teachback, of the learnings from this day. They can present in any way they like—encourage them to use their imaginations. They may use any of the materials given to them, and anything in the room. Make flip charts, etc. available. Ask for volunteers (no options!). Small teams or partners can work together. Let them know it would be ideal if everyone had an opportunity to do this, whether alone or in partnership with others. The only thing you ask is that they ably summarize all the day's learnings in 10 minutes. There are no other guidelines! *(Facilitators may wish to make this mandatory for entire group, split into teams, each team doing an original presentation in 2 minutes!)*

☐ Let volunteers know they will be presenting first thing the following morning. Thank them for their participation.

### PERSONAL REFLECTIONS (10 minutes)

☐ Refer participants to page 124 in the Participant Workbook. Explain that they will be given a few moments at the end of each day to **reflect and capture** their thoughts about what they have experienced and learned in the day. Remind them also to spend a few minutes on their **Leader Partner Feedback**. Do this now. *(Facilitator(s) may wish to write down a few of their own thoughts at this time as well, on the following page in this guide.)*

### COMMUNITY TIME (20 minutes)

**Challenge participants to:**
- apply what they have learned today immediately, even tonight, wherever, and with whomever.
- get the model "in your bones!"

☐ This serves as the day-end calibration time, allows for flexibility in time scheduling, and also makes an excellent use of Facilitator(s)' expertise. *(If you have deferred any questions that have come up during the day, this is the time to answer them.)*
  ☐ Encourage questions and answers.
  ☐ Encourage learning more about one another.
  ☐ Encourage sharing experiences, outstanding learnings, etc.
  ☐ **Encourage/discuss homework (page 21 Participant Workbook)**
  ☐ Continue informal conversation until close of day.

### DAY 1 CLOSE

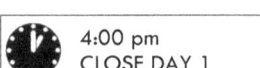

> 4:00 pm
> CLOSE DAY 1

# Day 1 - Personal Notes — Facilitator

*Use this page to record any notes you have about your facilitation of Day 1 of the Institute*

# Day 2

# Day 2 – Overview — Morning

| SESSION | CLOCK | TIME ALLOTED | ACTIVITY | DETAILS |
|---|---|---|---|---|
| **1** INTRO/REVIEW (9:00-9:40) 40 | 9:00-9:05 | 5 minutes | WELCOME | Good morning and welcome back! General welcome time. |
| | 9:05-9:20 | 15 minutes | TEACHBACK AND DISCUSSION | Volunteer(s) deliver(s) teachback of previous Day's learnings, with follow-up brief discussion, questions. This is intended to quick and laser-like. |
| | 9:20-9:30 | 10 minutes | DEBRIEF HOMEWORK | Ask for participants' insights, feedback regarding homework. Do not spend too much time on this. |
| | 9:30-9:40 | 10 minutes | QUICK LL REVIEW | Very fast review of Legacy Leadership and the 5 Best Practices. Make use of model to review the 5 Best Practices before content delivery on these. |
| **2** Best Practice #1 (9:40—10:50 - break) 1 hr 10 | 9:40-9:50 | 10 minutes | BP 1—DEFINING THE TERMS EXCERCISE | Ask participants to provide their own definitions of all 3 terms associated with BP1—HOLDER, VISION, VALUES. Ask for examples of a holder, a vision, values. Discuss meanings, applications. Have them document in Journal. |
| | 9:50-10:05 | 15 minutes | BP1—CONTENT DELIVERY | Deliver content of BP 1 with Field Guide (other matls etc.), personal experiences, as you would share it informally, or with corporate group. (Use "teachpoints") |
| | 10:05-10:15 | 10 minutes | BP1—"HOW TO" and "IMPORTANT PIECES" EXERCISES (Preparation) | Using Behaviors and Competencies bullets for BP 1, assign 2 or 3 bullets to each person/group (at least 1 each for vision and values). Divide up between the participants. Have them use their Participant Workbooks, experiences, former and current learnings to provide a "HOW TO" guide to accomplish these bullet points. Each one will report back after break. They may use any method desired to present, but should answer the question, "how is this accomplished in the workplace?" Refer also to the "Puzzle" page following (7 most important pieces of BP1). |
| | 10:15-10:30 | 15 minutes | BREAK | Informal, in room or out |
| | 10:30-10:45 | 15 minutes | BP1 "HOW TO" DEBRIEF and DISCUSS | Each person/group reports back steps for accomplishing assigned bullet points, allow group comment. This should be done quickly. Keep track of time! |
| | 10:45-10:50 | 5 minutes | BP1 "IMPORTANT PIECES" DEBRIEF and DISCUSS | Debrief the "Important Pieces" of the BP1 Puzzle. Share individual determinations of the 7 most important pieces necessary for the whole picture (selected from the bullet points.) |
| **3** Best Practice #5 (10:50—11:30) 40 min | 10:50-10:55 | 5 minutes | BP5—SET UP (THE OTHER BOOKEND PRACTICE) | Quickly introduce BP 5 as the paired bookend to BP 1. Explain the concept of BP1 and BP5 being the bookends of Legacy Leadership, and why. Use stories, drama, visual aids, object lessons to illustrate. |
| | 10:55-11:05 | 10 minutes | BP5—DEFINING THE TERMS EXCERCISE | Ask participants to suggest their own definitions of all three terms associated with BP5—CALIBRATOR, RESPONSIBILITY, ACCOUNTABILITY. Ask for examples of a calibrator, what is responsibility, accountability, etc. Discuss meanings, applications. (visual aids, object lessons, etc.). Participants record notes. |
| | 11:05-11:20 | 15 minutes | BP5—CONTENT DELIVERY EXERCISE (preparation) | Participants are now the facilitators and you are the learners. Give 15 minutes to prepare by using their Participant Workbook and any other materials to teach you (the facilitators) about BP 5. (Any way they want, but as a team) Tell them to use the foundational concepts of LL. |
| | 11:20-11:30 | 10 minutes | BP5—CONTENT DELIVERY (by participants) | Have participants teach you the content of BP5. You can have prepared or spontaneous questions to ask, as if you were the learner, and they the teachers. |

Day 2 MORNING continued next page...

# Day 2 - Overview — Morning, continued

| SESSION | CLOCK | TIME ALLOTED | ACTIVITY | DETAILS |
|---|---|---|---|---|
| **4** Bridging Gap BP1-5 (11:30-12:00) 30 | 11:30-11:50 | 20 minutes | **BRIDGING THE GAP BETWEEN BP 1 AND BP 5—OPEN DISCUSSION** | Most difficult part of these two BPs is bridging the gap between them. How do you go from vision to measurement and accountability? Ask for suggestions. Participants share thoughts and ideas, experiences and record on provided worksheet. Add to lists for what a leader must know, believe, do. *(this can be done on all BPs if desired)* INTRODUCE "MAPPING THE PLAN" as method of bridging the gap. Discuss. |
| | 11:50-12:00 | 10 minutes | **OBSERVATIONS AND INSIGHTS— Calibration** | Spend last few minutes before lunch debriefing insights, observations, personal applications, questions etc. (can also be used as flex time for activities). Calibration. |

*Day 2 continued next page... (AFTERNOON)*

# Day 2 - Overview — Afternoon

| SESSION | CLOCK | TIME ALLOTED | ACTIVITY | DETAILS |
|---|---|---|---|---|
| | 12:00-1:00 | 1 hour | LUNCH | In or out (depending on facility) |
| **5** Best Practice #3 (1:00-1:40) 40 min | 1:00-1:05 | 5 minutes | BP3—SET UP | Introduce BP 3 as the heart of Legacy Leadership, explain why. Use object lessons, visual aids, stories, etc. to illustrate. |
| | 1:05-1:15 | 10 minutes | BP3 - DEFINING THE TERMS EXERCISE | Definitions of all 3 terms associated with BP3—INFLUENCER, INSPIRATION, LEADERSHIP. Discuss meanings, applications. *(Use alternative methods to discuss these definitions—see Guide.)* |
| | 1:15-1:25 | 10 minutes | BP3—CONTENT DELIVERY | Using the Participant Workbook, go over basics. This is intended to be a quick delivery, based on printed info and your experiences. |
| | 1:25-1:40 | 15 minutes | BP3—WHAT DOES THE INFLUENTIAL LEADER LOOK LIKE? | Use large chart of unisex body outline. What does influential leader look like, do etc. Think of leaders (bosses, public personality, teacher, coach, etc.) who influenced them. What about person influenced them and continues to do so? What did they do? etc. (see Guide) Quickly capture in bullets on chart. (Class can do writing on board, or large sheets of paper, and LJ.) Underscore: Legacy Leaders, real leaders, never forget they are leaders. |
| **6** Situational Story Development (SSD) (1:40-3:30 -break) 1 hr 35 min | 1:40-1:50 | 10 minutes | SSD— SEGUE + SET-UP | Segue with story (modified case study-see Guide). Define situational storytelling; show how story has illustrated this. |
| | 1:50-2:05 | 15 minutes | ANATOMY OF STORY | Why is situational storytelling an effective tool? Review Participant Workbook, Analyze "Two Seeds" story in FAC Guide. Point out 7 elements of a story. |
| | 2:05-2:15 | 10 minutes | SSD EXERCISE (Set-up and Preparation) | Power of professional experience developed into stories for business application. Explain exercise, allow brief time before break to prepare individual stories using 7-element bullet outline. |
| | 2:15-2:30 | 15 minutes | BREAK | Informal, in or out |
| | 2:30-2:45 | 15 minutes | SSD EXERCISE (Presentations) | After break, allow additional time of preparation, then presentation of volunteer stories, critique and feedback, discussion. |
| | 2:45-3:00 | 15 minutes | ADAPTING OTHER STORIES EXERCISE (Preparation) | Exercise adapting stories of others, those found in publication, etc. for individual professional use. Exercise involves using popular business periodicals, finding relevant article/item of interest, preparing 2-minute story using 7-elements. |
| | 3:00-3:10 | 10 minutes | ADAPTING STORIES (Presentations) | Participants share stories with a partner, offer feedback, discuss together. |
| | 3:10-3:15 | 5 minutes | ADAPTING Debrief | Quick debrief and discussion of this rich tool. Encourage continued use. |
| | 3:15-3:25 | 10 minutes | PERSONAL STORIES/ PROFESSIONAL APP. | Discussion and quick exercise, volunteer sharing of a personal experience developed for profession (business) application (like a parable). |
| | 3:25-3:00 | 5 minutes | SSD RECAP | Very quick recap of SSD learnings, encouragement to make a habit and to continue collecting stories for influential use. |

# Day 2 - Overview
## Afternoon, continued

| SESSION | CLOCK | TIME ALLOTED | ACTIVITY | DETAILS |
|---|---|---|---|---|
| **7** Reflection/Wrap/Calibration (3:30-4:00) 30 min. | 3:30-3:35 | 5 minutes | **TEACHBACK VOLUNTEER** | Get tomorrow's teachback volunteer(s) to capture today's learnings, and make presentation (10 minutes) |
| | 3:35-3:45 | 10 minutes | **PERSONAL REFLECTION** | Capture Day 2's key learnings, personal reflection, in Participant Workbook. Leader Partner Feedback. |
| | 3:45-4:00 | 15 minutes | **COMMUNITY TIME (Calibration)** | Time for questions and answers, learning more about each other, questioning of experts, sharing experiences, outstanding learnings, etc. Explain briefly Day 2's more in-depth focus on the BPs. Address any questions not immediately relevant to the activities at hand earlier in the day, to this time. Also, you may want to tell more stories during this time. (Calibration time). |
| | 4:00 | | **CLOSE DAY 2** | Thank everyone for a great day! |

## Day 2 SUMMARY

**Morning**
Session 2-1     Intro/Review                           40 minutes
Session 2-2     Best Practice #1                       1 hour 10 minutes
*Morning break in this session*
Session 2-3     Best Practice #5                       40 minutes
Session 2-4     Bridging the Gap BP1-5                 30 minutes
*Lunch*


**Afternoon**
Session 2-5     Best Practice #3                       40 minutes
Session 2-6     Situational Storytelling Development   1 hour 35 minutes
*Afternoon break in this session*
Session 2-7     Wrap/Calibration                       30 minutes
*Close*

# Day 2 — PREPARATION

**PREPARATION**

No additional preparation is required for the morning session. Participants need Participant Workbooks, pencils, pens, flip charts, etc.

FOR AFTERNOON:

- ☐ Large chart with outline of a body (can be pre-made, or drawn on large white board, chalkboard, or butcher paper)

- ☐ Collected business periodicals for Situational Story Development module

# Day 2 — TARGET GOALS

## GOALS FOR MORNING SESSION, DAY 2

### Session 2-1: Intro
- Welcome back
- Teachback and Discussion
- Debrief Homework
- Quick Legacy Leadership/Best Practices Review

This is a warm-up session to begin the morning. Days 2 and 3 will begin this way. The intention is to continue to get to know one another better, to provide for interaction in teachbacks and to quickly debrief the homework. Facilitator allows teachback and quick discussion, followed by questions regarding the homework. Last night's homework was to "make a case" for Legacy Leadership using the Business Imperative. These exercises serve as a way to deepen the Legacy Leadership experience, utilizing the participant's own time, rather than Institute time. This morning debrief acts as a calibration of those times. In addition, a very quick review of the Best Practices serves as a reminder and a segue to the delivery of content about the 5 Best Practices.

### Session 2-2: Best Practice #1
- Defining the Terms Exercise
- BP1 Content Delivery
- BP1 "How To" Exercise
- BP1 "Important Pieces" Exercise

This session is designed to bring the participant to a new level of understanding of Best Practice 1—Holder of Vision and Values™. This is accomplished through defining the terms (HOLDER, VISION, VALUES) walking through the Field Guide definitions and distinctions in more detail, sharing personal experiences, reviewing teachpoints, and allowing participants to give some thought to how this BP is actually accomplished in the work place. The "puzzle exercise" asks participants to look at the key pieces and their relationship in the "whole picture" view of this best practice.

### Session 2-3: Best Practice #5
- Set-Up Best Practice #5—The "Other Bookend"
- BP5—Defining the Terms Exercise
- BP5—Content Delivery Exercise (participants)

Best Practice #5—Calibrator of Responsibility and Accountability™— is presented immediately after Best Practice #1, to show their relationship and the "bookend" qualities of vision and accountability for that vision. This session's goals are to present the content of this best practice for a new level of understanding (expanding on previous day's information) and to provide participants an opportunity to teach themselves and others.

### Session 2-4: Bridging the Gap Between BP1 and BP5
- Bridging the Gap—Open Discussion
- Observations and Insights (Calibration time)

This session is designed to show the gap that exists in most businesses between these two best practices, and share open discussion about how this can be bridged. Best Practice 5 is perhaps the hardest of all to actually practice successfully. The "Mapping the Plan" form and concept is introduced as a helpful tool in this endeavor. This time is open discussion with sharing of experiences and suggestions for success. The calibration time serves as providing time flexibility, and acts as a debrief opportunity for previous learnings. These "calibration" times are provided frequently throughout the Institute. They are opportunities for personal interaction and continued content delivery on an informal basis.

*Goals continued, next page...*

# Day 2: TARGET GOALS

**GOALS FOR AFTERNOON SESSION, DAY 2**

### Session 2-5: Best Practice #3
- Set-Up as "Heart" of Legacy Leadership
- BP3—Defining the Terms Exercise
- BP3—Content Delivery
- BP3—What does the Influential Leader Look Like?

Best Practice #3—Influencer of Inspiration and Leadership™—is presented next as the "heart" of Legacy Leadership®. This session is intended to impart not only the content of this best practice, but the heart of having people and others as its foundational center. Defining the Terms Exercise is provided for in all the best practices. This content delivery method is standard, through use of the Field Guide and other materials. In addition, the participants are encouraged to honestly look at just what an influential leader looks like and relate that to this best practice.

### Session 2-6: Situational Storytelling Development (SSD)
- Segue and Set-Up
- Anatomy of a Story
- Situational Story Development Exercise (Set-Up)
- Situational Story Development Exercise (Presentations)
- Adapting Other Stories Exercise (Prep)
- Adapting Other Stories Exercise (Presentations)
- Personal Stories with Professional Application
- Situational Stories Recap

This session is designed to provide the participant with a powerful tool (and hopefully a lifelong habit) to enhance their influential leadership and develop other leaders. It is inserted here as a tie-in to best practice #3. Good stories come from the heart, and BP3 is about the heart of the leader, the heart of Legacy Leadership®, and influencing others. Through a variety of exercises which include using professional and personal stories, and adapting stories from other sources, participants are given a solid foundation and skills on which to build their own repertoire of situational stories.

This session is all about leaders solving complex business problems, influencing and inspiring others, overcoming obstacles. In short, bringing out the best in people through stories developed for specific situational applications. The purpose of this module for Legacy Leadership® is to build the skills for leaders to communicate a message that influences and inspires buy-in and commitment to vision or other communicated messages.

*NOTE: This SSD Module is intentionally designed "tight" and needs to be facilitated well with the overall time guides in mind, as well as sensitivity to what is happening within the group.*

### Session 2-7: Reflection/Wrap/Calibration
- Teachback Volunteer(s)
- Personal Reflection
- Community Time (Calibration time)

This is time to enlist volunteers for teachbacks, participant reflection and Leader Partner feedback, and to address issues that have come up during the day's learnings. Facilitator(s) also reminds of homework and need for leader feedback. This time is flexible, at Facilitator discretion. *Serves as calibration time for the day, as well as a time flexibility slot.*

# Day 2 - Morning — Session 2-1

**SESSION 2-1: INTRO**

🕐 9:00 am—9:40 am
40 Min.

- Welcome back
- Teachback and Discussion
- Debrief Homework
- LL/5 Best Practices Review

*(Suggested times shown in parentheses after heading)*

**WELCOME (5 minutes)**

☐ Welcome participants back to another Day of Legacy Learning!

**TEACHBACK AND DISCUSSION (15 minutes)**

☐ **Introduce volunteer(s) doing teachback.** Give them the floor for approximately 10 minutes to teach back, in whatever method they choose, the learnings from Day 1.

☐ Facilitate a **brief discussion about the teachback** and take any remaining questions about Day 1. Keep this quick and laser like. Watch the clock!

**DEBRIEF HOMEWORK (10 minutes)**

☐ Ask participants to **share their insights regarding the homework** (to read through the **Business Applications for Legacy Leadership**® section of the Participant Workbook and "make a case" for Legacy Leadership®.) Discuss their experiences, findings, learnings. Remember this is not a "marketing" exercise, but one to familiarize participants and deepen their overall understanding of Legacy Leadership so that they will be able to successfully discuss its foundations and benefits within their group or organization. Indicate how important this exercise is to their own application.

**QUICK REVIEW OF BEST PRACTICES OF LEGACY LEADERSHIP® (10 minutes)**

☐ Indicate that today will be spent covering three of the five Best Practices. Ask participants to look at the Legacy Leadership model printed on the back of the Participant Workbook, and pages 150 and 151. Briefly cover the information there.

☐ Explain that the **terms** (the language) used to label each Best Practice were chosen deliberately to evoke some thought and remembrance of these best practices. Explain the importance of understanding each of these terms fully and how each term becomes an integral part of the best practice.

# Day 2 - Morning — Sessions 2-1, 2-2

**SESSION 2-1: INTRO continued**

**QUICK BP OVERVIEW (continued)**

☐ Each best practice is **composed of three parts:**
- The action descriptor, which is the BEING of the best practice
- The two intended results descriptors, which is the DOING of the best practice

For example: Best Practice #1 is Holder of Vision and Values™. HOLDER is the **BEING** part of this best practice (who they ARE), and the Vision and Values are the DOING part (what they DO). The successful practice of each of these is dependent upon understanding each separate part to make the whole, and the fact that a *Legacy Leader* practices BEING and DOING both parts, not just one.

☐ Be sure **all 5 Best Practices are discussed** in this brief overview. Be thorough but quick. Watch the clock!

**SESSION 2-2: BEST PRACTICE #1**

 9:40 am—10:50 am
1 Hour 10 minutes

**DEFINING THE TERMS EXERCISE (10 minutes)**

- BP1—Defining the Terms Exercise
- BP1 Content Delivery
- BP1 "How To" and "Important Pieces" Exercises
- MORNING BREAK
- BP1 "How To" Exercise Report Back
- BP1 "Important Pieces" Exercise Report Back

*(Suggested times shown in parentheses after heading)*

☐ Direct participants to page 25 of their Participant Workbooks. Ask participants to provide their own definitions of all 3 terms associated with BP1—HOLDER, VISION, VALUES™. Give them a few minutes to think and write, then ask for examples, object lessons, metaphors, etc. Discuss meanings, understandings, applications to BP1. *(Be careful not to allow this discussion to get out of hand. Do not allow this "defining" exercise to go beyond the allotted 10 minutes.)*

**BP 1 CONTENT DELIVERY (15 minutes)**

☐ This may be accomplished at the Facilitator(s)' discretion. Facilitator should be fully prepared in advance by reading the section of the Field Guide that pertains to BP1. It is suggested that facilitators refer to the Model frequently. If desired, take participants to the Field Guide for <u>quick</u> content review.

☐ It may not be feasible or even desirable to completely read through all the material presented in the Field Guide, or any other materials. Be sure participants are familiar with it, however, and encourage them to review in depth on their own.

# Day 2 - Morning — Session 2-2

**SESSION 2-2: BEST PRACTICE #1 continued**

**BP 1 CONTENT DELIVERY (continued)**

☐ This should be an **informal discussion**, not necessarily a "lecture" format. Be sure to impart the basics of this best practice, including the teach points below. *(These are an elaboration of the points found on the back of the Model.)*

### BP1 Main Teach Points — BP 1

(Found on back of LL Model)

1. **Keep vision and values clear**—A leader knows and can articulate his or her own and the organization's vision and values, lives by them and builds them into the overall vision – everyday. Vision and values are non-negotiable.

2. **Sustain focus and clarity**—This is easier to do in good times, but a true Legacy Leader sustains focus and clarity through good times and bad. In fact, strong leadership is needed even more when times are tough; teams are faced with fear or uncertainty and are looking to the leader to provide clarity and focused energy.

3. **Develop and execute strategy**—Once the leader is grounded in vision and values, the next step is to translate these high level pictures into executable plans. These strategies provide the roadmap for the organization to achieve the long-term visions.

4. **Establish the measurables**—This is designing the metrics to measure success. Some key elements of good metrics include being specific – what does success look like? How will we know it when we see it? Next, they need to be measurable and quantifiable and have a reasonable probability of achievement, while stretching at the same time. Lastly, there needs to be a time element, not only to create urgency but to ensure expectations are clear with everyone. These milestones also provide the opportunity to celebrate small successes along the way as well as recognize the final success.

5. **Gain commitment to action**—Legacy Leaders® inspire others with vision that is shared by everyone. The picture of the future is so attractive and clear that all parties are eager to be part of it. Gaining personal commitment will ensure that the vision and the strategies come to fruition.

*Facilitator Note: In our delivery of the 5 Best Practices, we have found that with encouragement and a review of the printed materials, most groups actually teach this material themselves through group discussion. We suggest facilitators watch for this and encourage it. You may only need to fill in any gaps in understanding. As always, however, be careful to watch the clock and not allow discussions to extend into other delivery time.*

☐ **RECOMMENDED:** Any content is always more readily learned through powerful stories. The Facilitator should be prepared in advance to share a story from their own (or others') experience that is an example, or illustrates, Best Practice #1.

☐ If time allows, explain that BP1 is not only about HAVING Vision and holding it, but being able to **TRANSLATE and ADAPT an existing corporate Vision (Mission)** into terms applicable to individuals, teams, and groups within the organization.

☐ NOTE: While Vision is often easier to discuss, **do not neglect the VALUES** portion of this best practice.

# Day 2 - Morning  Session 2-2

**SESSION 2-2: BEST PRACTICE #1 continued**

**BP1"HOW TO"/ IMPORTANT PIECES EXERCISE (preparation—10 minutes)**

- ☐ Refer participants to page 26 of the Participant Workbook (Competencies and Behaviors). Assign 2 or 3 bullets (at least one each for vision and values) to each person. Divide all bullet points up between the participants (some may do the same ones, depending on number in group).

- ☐ Instruct participants to use their Participant Workbooks, their experiences, their former and current learnings to provide a "HOW TO" guide to accomplish these bullet points. They may use any method desired (song, skit, teaching, etc.—be creative!) to do this, but they MUST answer the question: HOW IS THIS ACCOMPLISHED IN THE WORKPLACE?

- ☐ In addition to this exercise, refer them to the next page in their workbooks, page 27, where they will find a graphic of a puzzle. There are 7 pieces. Ask them to label the pieces with what they consider to be the 7 most important behaviors necessary to the "whole picture" of BP1. This should be done during this same preparation time and will be reported back after the break.

**MORNING BREAK (15 minutes)**

**BP1 "HOW TO" EXERCISE DELIVERY AND DISCUSSION (15 minutes)**

> 10:15 am—10:30 am
> BREAK 15 minutes

- ☐ Each participant/group reports (or sings, dances, teaches, etc.!) their methods for accomplishing their assigned bullet points in the workplace. Discuss as opportune. This should be done quickly. Keep track of time here! *(NOTE: depending on class size and number of participants at each table group, you may choose to have them work and report out as groups rather than individuals. Decide this in advance, and be sure to keep groups on task mindful of time used.)*

**BP1 "IMPORTANT PIECES" EXERCISE REPORT BACK (5 minutes)**

- ☐ Ask participants to share their findings for the "Important Pieces" exercise. Which top 7 pieces did they choose? Why? Discuss briefly. Facilitator provides guidance and personal experience.

# Day 2 - Morning — Session 2-3

**SESSION 2-3: BEST PRACTICE #5**

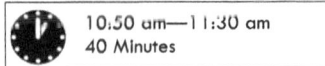
10:50 am—11:30 am
40 Minutes

**BP5—THE "OTHER BOOKEND" SET-UP (5 minutes)**

- BP5 Set-Up
- BP5—Defining the Terms Exercise
- BP5—Content Delivery Exercise

☐ **Quickly introduce BP5 as the paired bookend to BP1.** Explain this concept of BP1 and BP5 being the bookends of Legacy Leadership®, and why.

*(Suggested times shown in parentheses after heading)*

☐ **RECOMMENDED:** Once again, a powerful story, visual aid or other memorable way to illustrate the importance of BP 5 as the mate to BP1 is highly suggested. Facilitator should prepare this in advance and deliver quickly and powerfully.

**DEFINING THE TERMS EXERCISE (10 minutes)**

☐ Direct participants to page 35 of their Participant Workbook. Ask them to provide their own **definitions** of all 3 terms associated with BP5—CALIBRATOR, RESPONSIBILITY, and ACCOUNTABILITY™. Give them a few minutes to think and write, then ask for examples, object lessons, metaphors, etc. Discuss meanings, understandings, applications to BP5. (*Facilitator NOTE: It is also suggested that this "defining" exercise at the beginning of each BP delivery be varied somewhat for each. For example, you may choose to have the participants swap Participant Workbooks and write their own definitions in a partner's journal and then the partner reads the entries. Or you may ask for – or even assign – quick impromptu "charades" to define these terms. Or have them "draw" the term instead of write it on the page—even on butcher paper or white boards for everyone to see. [This can work something like the game "Pictionary."] Use your imagination and stimulating thought provokers. Whatever you do, be sure to keep track of your time and don't allow this exercise to take up content delivery time.*)

**BP5 CONTENT DELIVERY EXERCISE (Preparation)**
**(15 minutes)**

☐ Explain to participants that **they are now the teachers**, and you are the learner. This is their opportunity to "get into" the content of BP5 on their own, and prepare to "teach" you. Give them 15 minutes to prepare, using any materials they have available (Participant Workbooks, their own experiences, any props you have provided, etc.) to teach you the content of Best Practice 5. The <u>whole group</u> must act as a TEAM, and delivery can be in any format they choose, as long as the main content and foundational concepts of BP5 are presented in a way that promotes real learning. (They will have 10 minutes to make their presentation following preparation.) Direct them to use page 37 in the Participant Workbook to write down ideas.

# Day 2 - Morning
## Session 2-4

**SESSION 2-4: BRIDGING THE GAP BETWEEN BP1 AND BP5**

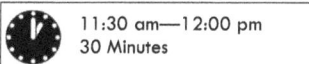
11:30 am—12:00 pm
30 Minutes

**BRIDGING THE GAP BETWEEN BP1 AND BP5—OPEN DISCUSSION (20 minutes)**

- Bridging the Gap—Open Discussion
- Observations and Insights (Calibration time)

*(Suggested times shown in parentheses after heading)*

☐ Open this discussion by explaining that **BP5 is a critical** best practice and **almost always forgotten**. Ask how they go from vision to measurement and accountability? Ask for suggestions on how this is accomplished, and actual experiences of the learners. Have participants share thoughts and ideas.

☐ Explore the question: **Where is legacy found here?** Facilitate very quick responses and discussion around legacy and these best practices.

☐ If necessary, or desired, add any thoughts to the chart that depicts what a leader must KNOW, BELIEVE and DO.

☐ Direct participants to page 38 in the Participant Workbook **"Mapping the Plan for Organizational Results"** and offer it as a method of bridging this gap. Discuss quickly. They will have further opportunity to use this tool again in the Development Planning session on Day 3, so don't spend a lot of time here.


**OBSERVATIONS AND INSIGHTS (Calibration time)**
**(10 minutes)**

☐ Following the discussion on bridging the gap, if time allows, spend the last few minutes before lunch debriefing what has been discussed about BP1 and BP5, and the potential gap between them. Ask for insights, new observations, personal applications, questions, etc. (This time is also intended for time flexibility, and a period of calibration.)


**LUNCH (1 hour)**

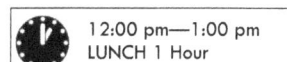
12:00 pm—1:00 pm
LUNCH 1 Hour

# Day 2 - Morning — Session 2-4

**BP5 CONTENT DELIVERY EXERCISE (Presentation)**
**(10 minutes)**

☐ **Call group back to order** when 15 minutes is up. Give them the floor, sit back, and let them impart their newly found wisdom about BP5. If necessary, debrief and fill in any gaps. (Use Main Teach Points chart below if needed.)

## BP5 Main Teach Points

(Found on back of LL Model)

1. **Execute strategies well with implemented action plans**—The leader is constantly "trimming the sails," making adjustments to strategies and actions to improve performance and results.

2. **Have vigilant awareness of progress towards goals**—A Legacy Leader® is always mindful of where the team is at relative to the goals and timelines. Vigilance and ongoing checkpoints keep everyone focused on the same end result.

3. **Require peak performance, support and buy-in from all**—This is not "command and control" or providing orders without context – gaining buy-in from all affected parties ensures that there is absolute clarity and commitment.

4. **Have clear consistent accountabilities, follow-through**—Everyone knows what role they play – the specific actions and expectations along with consequences and rewards – to the individual and the organization.

5. **Be aware of trends, adapt to change and recalibrate as necessary**—No plan is stagnant, constant monitoring and recalibrating keeps a direct and clear vision in the sight of everyone, not just the leader.

*Facilitator Note: Allow a few moments to discuss any questions that arise.*

*Immediately following this presentation, move onto session 2-4...*

# Day 2 - Afternoon — Session 2-5

**SESSION 2-5: BEST PRACTICE #3**

1:00 pm—1:40 pm
40 minutes

**BP3 SET-UP (5 minutes)**

- BP3 Set-Up
- BP3 Defining the Terms Exercise
- BP3 Content Delivery
- BP3—What does the Influential Leader Look Like?

☐ Introduce **BP3 as the "heart" of Legacy Leadership®**, explain why. This best practice is about relationships, and breathes life into all the others. *(Reminder: Use stories, visual aids, or other memorable pieces to illustrate these concepts.)*

*(Suggested times shown in parentheses after heading)*

**BP3 DEFINING THE TERMS EXERCISE (10 minutes)**

☐ Direct participants to page 41 of their Participant Workbook. Ask participants to provide their own **definitions** of all 3 terms associated with BP3—INFLUENCER, INSPIRATION, LEADERSHIP™. Give them a few minutes to think and write, then ask for examples, object lessons, metaphors, etc. *(Reminder: Be sure to use various methods to facilitate this exercise.)* Discuss meanings, understandings, applications to BP3.

**BP3 DELIVERY CONTENT (10 minutes)**

☐ This may be accomplished at the Facilitator(s)' discretion, using either Field Guide or Model. An effective overview is the Aerial View (can be used for all or some BP delivery content, but should be pointed out to participants) in the Field Guide. (Again, it may not be feasible to read all material—encourage learners to do this on their own.) This is intended to be a quick overview of the basics. *(Use key points included here.)*

## BP3 Main Teach Points

*(Found on back of LL Model)*

1. **Build positive, meaningful relationships with energy**—The leader knows the value of personal connection, showing genuine care and concern for others and actively building, maintaining and nurturing relationships – for the sake of the relationship only.

2. **Place leadership emphasis on people for positive outcomes**—By building on strengths and learning from mistakes, individuals are raised up with every encounter with the Legacy Leader. There is no ego or self focus – the energy and emphasis is on positive outcomes – where everyone wins.

3. **Recognize, acknowledge and inspire others**—The Legacy Leader® is dedicated to gaining results by recognizing and sharing the accomplishments of others. There is no "I", there is only "We." The Leader succeeds ONLY if the team and individuals succeed.

4. **Enable others to lead through positive modeling**—This is about "walking the talk" when it comes to inspiring and leading others – when looking up at the Legacy Leader®, are the actions and behaviors aligned with the speeches and statements?

5. **Be humble, with a fierce resolve for each person's success**—Check the ego at the door. True Legacy Leaders® are recharged and gain personal satisfaction through the successes of others. Humility is about not knowing all the answers, admitting mistakes and aiming the spotlight on others.

# Day 2 - Afternoon — Session 2-5

**SESSION 2-5: BEST PRACTICE #3 continued**

**WHAT DOES THE INFLUENTIAL LEADER LOOK LIKE?**
**(15 minutes)**

- ☐ Use a **pre-made large outline of a body** (unisex!) on a large piece of butcher paper, or chalkboard, etc. Direct group to Participant Workbook, page 42 where they can record their own observations.

- ☐ Ask the group **what an influential leader looks** like, what that person does that makes them inspirational/influential. If desired, you may relate the parts of the body to various best practices, if the discussion goes in that direction (i.e., head = BP1, heart = BP3, etc.).

- ☐ Ask learners to **think of leaders** (bosses, public personalities, teachers, coaches, etc.) who influenced them in life.
    - What about that person influenced them and continues to do so?
    - What in particular did he or she do that inspired/influenced you?
    - How did that make them connect so powerfully with others?

    Quickly capture in 1-2 word bullets on chart. *(OPTION: If feasible, you may choose to have participants divide into table groups, or other designated groups to mix them up, and go to pre-drawn outlines on butcher paper posted around the room to do this themselves and debrief each one.)*

- ☐ Quickly **refer learners back to the "Know-Believe-Do"** 3-column chart they built earlier. How does this compare to that chart? Does anything need to be added to either chart?

- ☐ Relate these observations to BP3.

- ☐ Underscore that a Legacy Leader® never forgets he or she is a leader, and why this is important. Underscore the importance of BEING an influencer.

# Day 2 - Afternoon — Session 2-6

**SESSION 2-6: SITUATIONAL STORY DEVELOPMENT (SSD)**

 1:40 pm—3:30 pm
1 hour 50 minutes

**SEGUE TO SITUATIONAL STORYTELLING SET-UP**
**(10 minutes)**

- Segue to SSD Set-up
- Anatomy of a Story
- Situational Story Development Exercise (Set-Up)
- AFTERNOON BREAK
- SSD Exercise (Presentations)
- Adapting Other Stories (Prep)
- Adapting Other Stories (Presentations)
- Adapting other Stories Debrief
- Personal Stories with Professional Application
- SSD Recap

☐ **Continue into this session seamlessly** by saying, "Now I want to tell you a story." **Tell the following story**, or use another powerful story from your own experience. *(If you use your own story, be sure it follows the "Components of an Inspiring Story" found on page 44 of the Participant Workbook (and pages 47-48 this Guide), and that it is relevant to Legacy Leadership® and will lead to some brief discussion. The story used here is slightly retold from a Case Study that will be used later in the Institute, and is a true story.)*

*(Suggested times shown in parentheses after heading)*

TIMING NOTE: This SSD Module is intentionally designed "tight" and needs to be facilitated well, with the overall time guides in mind, as well as sensitivity to what is happening within the group.

***Facilitator Note:*** *You should become so familiar with these stories before the Institute that you can TELL them and not READ them!*

**STORY:**

I had a client, a young highly proficient corporate lawyer named Terry, who was very well regarded in his company. There were two other lawyers in his department, but he never saw them since their offices were offsite. Because Terry was so efficient, and because of the overlap of their work, his boss, Cody, kept Terry close by, almost sequestering him from the rest of the company. But Terry rarely even saw Cody, though Cody was good about praising his work.

What Cody did not know was that Terry is a people person, and was not happy working in isolation. Most of the time Terry felt alone, working in isolation. Cody, because he really doesn't know Terry well, also did not know that Terry has very strong leadership potential and really wanted to work within a group in a team environment. Terry was beginning to feel stifled, with no growth opportunity.

Besides being very proficient, Terry had also become an industry expert in the regulatory cases he handled for the company, making himself a very valuable commodity to his company. Cody believed that keeping Terry in this position of Counsel, and working in relative isolation was best for the company. After all, where else could they find anyone who could handle these issues for them as well as Terry could? Cody continued to keep his highly regarded Counselor in virtual seclusion from the rest of the world.

Terry was withering on the vine in this position, and he knew it. Something had to change soon, or Terry would be out the door and onto another company where all of his strengths were valued and he could be fully readied for leadership.

**STOP THE STORY HERE.**

☐ "I want to stop here." Ask participants to **put themselves in the positions of Terry and Cody.** What is going on here? Ask questions to facilitate brief discussion:
- How can this situation be remedied, for both Terry and Cody?
- How and what do Terry and Cody communicate in this situation?
- How would an "influential" leader behave (both Terry and Cody's positions)?

# Day 2 - Afternoon — Session 2-6

**SESSION 2-6: SITUATIONAL STORY DEVELOPMENT (SSD) continued**

**SEGUE TO SITUATIONAL STORYTELLING SET-UP**
**(continued)**

- ☐ At this time do a **very quick debrief**, a fast facilitation of some possible answers to these questions. Don't spend a lot of time here. Move on quickly. *(At some point someone may ask you what happened to Terry. Delay/defer your answer...)*

- ☐ **Stop the discussion** after about 5 minutes. This may even be done abruptly to get their attention. *(This particular story is also a Case Study which can be more thoroughly debriefed during Day 3's exercises. Don't worry about completely discussing every possible answer to these questions.)* Indicate that what you have done here is **facilitated problem solving** and learning by telling what we call a situational story. "I told you a story from my experience in order to influence you and teach you from that emotional connection." **This is situational story telling.**

  > Situational story telling is telling an effective and powerful story that is relevant to a particular situation, causing those told to internalize it, remember it, and use it as a catalyst for positive change, growth or solution.
  >
  > Situational story telling is using a story from the past to illustrate the present in order to enhance the future.

- ☐ We have just talked about **Best Practice #3, which is all about being an influencer**, about making a connection with people. One of the most impactful methods of influence is through the ability to tell a persuasive story that connects both with the heart as well as the head, and then translates into action. By hearing about Terry and Cody, you were drawn into their dilemma and whether you knew it or not, you were problem solving their situation. This story could have been used to facilitate actual problem solving in a corporate setting. We are going to spend some time now exploring and working on developing situational stories. Turn to page 44 in your Participant Workbook.

**ANATOMY OF A STORY (15 minutes)**

- ☐ **Ask participants:**
    - Why do you think it is important for leaders to tell stories?
    - Why are stories effective in business application?
  
  Hear answers and facilitate **very brief discussion**. Possible answers include:
    - Stories are easier to remember than facts, figures and statistics
    - Stories sometimes contain a lesson, moral or compelling message
    - Leaders who tell stories leave themselves open and vulnerable (more "real") - it's not about the ego or power of the storyteller
    - Charisma of the storyteller helps, but it's the story itself that creates lasting impact
    - In many cultures (and families), stories are passed down from generation to generation, helping to define history
    - Stories effect us not only intellectually, but on an emotional (sometimes even spiritual) level

# Day 2 - Afternoon — Session 2-6

**SESSION 2-6: SITUATIONAL STORY DEVELOPMENT (SSD) continued**

**ANATOMY OF A STORY (continued)**

- ☐ Review the **"Components of an Inspiring Story"** on page 44 of the Participant Workbook, including the seven elements of a story.

- ☐ Ask learners to **keep these points in mind** as you read the following story, slowly, with "flair:"

Two seeds lay side by side in the fertile spring soil.

The first seed said, "I want to grow! I want to send my roots deep into the soil beneath me and thrust my sprouts through the earth's crust above me...I want to unfurl my tender buds like banners to announce the arrival of spring... I want to feel the warmth of the sun on my face and blessing of the morning dew on my petals."

And so she grew.

The second seed said, "I am afraid. If I send my roots into the ground below, I don't know what I will encounter in the dark. If I push my way through the hard soil above me, I may damage my delicate sprouts...What if I let my buds open and a snail tries to eat them? And if I were to open my blossoms, a small child may pull me from the ground. No, it is much better for me to wait until it is safe."

And so she waited.

A yard hen scratching around in the early spring ground for food found the waiting seed and promptly ate it.

*From "A Little Sip of Chicken Soup for the Soul" 1997*

- ☐ **After reading, lead a <u>very</u> quick discussion** asking the learners to identify the elements of this particular story verbally. (Sample responses below)
    1. **Introduction and Setting of Characters:** two seeds in the spring
    2. **Explanation of state of affairs:** first seed decides whether or not it wants to grow, then decides to reach out
    3. **Initiating event; a problem:** second seed has a different view of growing
    4. **Emotional response OR statement of goal by the protagonist:** second seed has fear
    5. **Complicating actions:** seed waits
    6. **An outcome:** a hen finds the seed and eats it
    7. **Reactions to the outcome:** usually most laugh, such an abrupt ending

- ☐ **What made this story so powerful?**
    - short and simple
    - on the surface it has a straightforward message but could be analyzed and examined at many different levels
    - has a lesson about fear vs. risk-taking (or positive vs. negative) perspectives and consequences
    - uses humor
    - has a parable-like feel

# Day 2 - Afternoon  Session 2-6

**SESSION 2-6: STORYTELLING continued**

**SITUATIONAL STORY DEVELOPMENT EXERCISE (Set-up)**
**(10 minutes)**

- ☐ Situational stories are not always from actual "case studies" but the more relevant the story to the group told, the more memorable it may be. However, there are **many different ways to incorporate situational stories** as powerful tools used appropriately by the INFLUENTIAL leader.

- ☐ Effective situational **stories can be developed** from any of the following:
  - Professional experiences
  - Personal experiences
  - Stories told by others that impacted you
  - Gleanings from reading, researching, news reports, etc.
  
  Not all stories have to be invented or "written" by you. Many can be adapted or retold through different filters for the same situational impact.

- ☐ In the business world, however, perhaps the most effective and the most immediately relevant to your business applications are **your own professional experiences**. For that reason, this is where we are going to start. Refer participants to page 45 of their Participant Workbooks.

- ☐ We want you to spend some time **considering a memorable <u>professional</u> experience** (your own!), preferably one which can be used to illustrate or underscore one of the 5 Best Practices (any aspect of any best practice).

- ☐ Using the 7 elements of a story found on page 44 of the Participant Workbook, **outline your story as briefly as possible.** Consider how you might tell this story in 2 minutes or less, still making it impactful and memorable. Also consider a hypothetical or real business situation where you might be able to use this story to influence others.

- ☐ We're going to give you about 5 minutes here to consider your stories, and then we will take a 15 minute break. When break is over, please return promptly. We'll give you another 5 or 10 minutes to finish your preparation and then we'll be sharing stories.

**AFTERNOON BREAK (15 minutes)**

> 2:15 pm—2:30 pm
> BREAK 15 minutes

*Facilitator Note:* Timing for this break may need to be modified, depending on how close you are to the printed schedule. Participants can also be encouraged to work on their stories through the break time.

# Day 2 - Afternoon — Session 2-6

**SESSION 2-6: SITUATIONAL STORYTELLING continued**

**SITUATIONAL STORY DEVELOPMENT EXERCISE (Presentation) (15 minutes)**

- ☐ After the break, **allow participants to work on their stories** for about 5 more minutes. At that point, call the preparations to a halt, and ask for 3 or 4 volunteers who are ready to share.

- ☐ Allow each volunteer **ONLY 2 minutes to tell their story** to the group. Instruct them to be animated, and to tell the story as if they are in the situation they envisioned for the story. Give them visual cues on timing. Signal when they have 30 seconds left, then halt the story and ask the group for any comments. It is not necessary to do a critique, but it may be helpful to offer a few suggestions or accolades. (Tell learners that there is space on pages 48 and 49 of their Participant Workbooks to capture any thoughts regarding their stories or the stories of others.)

- ☐ **Congratulate the volunteers**, and all participants, and encourage them to continue this practice by working at building a repertoire of effective stories from their own professional experiences.

**ADAPTING OTHER STORIES EXERCISE (Preparation) (15 minutes)**

- ☐ (Move *immediately* into this segment.) It is not always necessary to develop stories from your own professional experiences. Sometimes we will read an article, or hear another story from a variety of sources that can be added to our library of situational stories for various applications.

- ☐ Go around (Facilitator or assistant) to the various table groups and leave a stack (enough for one for each participant at that table) of various popular business periodicals. Duplicate magazines at a table are fine.

- ☐ Have each participant **select one periodical**. Instruct them to scan the magazine quickly, looking for a brief story, article, quote or some factoid that can be easily retold, one that captures their interest and is relevant to a business application that may or may not directly relate to Legacy Leadership (but you can tell them they get extra points if it does!). They are to do the same exercise with these articles of choice as they did with their professional stories: follow the 7 elements bullet outline and **adapt the article to a 2-minute story** they can tell to someone else. Have them use page 48 in the Participant Workbook for their outline. Let them work quietly on this for 15 minutes. (Note: This time restraint may challenge some people! Tell them to do their best!)

*Facilitator Note: Begin collecting these periodicals well in advance of the Institute. Back and duplicate issues are fine. Select magazines or newspapers that offer some quickly read "glimpses" rather than very lengthy articles, or a mix of both. Here's some suggestions for periodicals:*

- *The Wall Street Journal*
- *Harvard Business Review*
- *US News and World Report*
- *Newsweek*
- *Time*
- *Fortune*
- *Business Week*
- *Forbes*
- *The Economist*
- *Folio*
- *Business 20*
- *Entrepreneur*
- *Inc. Magazine*
- *National Review*
- *Women in Business*
- *Fast Company*
- *Success*
- *Executive Leadership*
- *Or any others appropriate to your group!*

# Day 2 - Afternoon — Session 2-6

**SESSION 2-6: SITUATIONAL STORYTELLING continued**

**ADAPTING OTHER STORIES (Presentation) (10 minutes)**

*Facilitator Note: Your storytelling sessions may require more than the time allotted here. Be sure to adjust your end-of-day schedule if this is the case. There is some flexibility here.*

- ☐ When the 15 minutes of preparation are up, ask the participants to grab their periodicals and their Participant Workbooks, go across the room to another table and **choose a partner** (they MUST change tables). Allow them a few noisy minutes to do this and settle them back down quickly.

- ☐ Tell learners to **take turns telling their adapted story** to their partner. They must tell it as if the partner is a co-worker or a group of team members involved in some situation to which the story pertains. Advise them to time each other, and not go beyond the 2-minute mark.

- ☐ After one partner shares, instruct the other to **critique and offer suggestions, comments or observations**. The other partner then shares his or her story, with feedback from the listener. Be sure participants know they have only 10 minutes in which to do this exercise. (If necessary, and if room allows, you may have the pairs move to areas of the room where their conversation can be more private.)

**ADAPTING OTHER STORIES EXERCISE (Debrief) (5 minutes)**

- ☐ When the time has expired for sharing stories with partners, ask the participants to **return to their normal seats.**

- ☐ Spend about **5 minutes debriefing** what they just did. Ask for comments about how comfortable they felt doing this and how they can practice this habit of continually gleaning their own stories from other stories. Discuss how this is effective in business application (not only transferring information, but making it relevant to a situation and a useful tool for problem solving, change, influence, etc.) Encourage them to find and use stories that illustrate Legacy Leadership®.

**PERSONAL STORIES WITH PROFESSIONAL APPLICATION (10 minutes)**

- ☐ (*Move immediately into this segment.*) Sometimes a personal experience, or that of a friend or acquaintance can have the most profound professional application. In these cases, these stories become like parables, where a point is made with memorable impact.

- ☐ For example, the **story of the seeds** we read a little while ago has no apparent or immediate business relevance, but could be very effectively used to make a point about waiting to make decisions, or playing it too safe instead of taking well-calculated risks for growth. In the same way, a particularly moving, dramatic, humorous or emotionally stimulating personal experience can be an extremely effective business tool.

▶

# Day 2 - Afternoon — Session 2-6

**SESSION 2-6: SITUATIONAL STORYTELLING continued**

**PERSONAL STORIES WITH PROFESSIONAL APPLICATION (continued)**

- ☐ Ask participants to reflect for a few moments about any particularly **memorable personal experiences** they have, or that they have personal knowledge of from others. Give them 5 minutes to think about this, and instruct them to **outline such an experience in the 7 elements format**, with the additional task of determining **how this story can be effective in a particular business situation**. Ask them to jot down their thoughts in the note pages of the Participant Workbook under the storytelling section.

- ☐ After about 5-7 minutes, **ask for volunteers to share** such an experience, in a 2-minute story format. Hear as many volunteers as time allows, and as are willing to share.

- ☐ Thank the volunteers for sharing, debrief and **recap how personal stories can be very powerful business tools** for the influential leader.

**SITUATIONAL STORIES RECAP (5 minutes)**

- ☐ Spend the last few minutes of this session discussing what the **participants have learned about situational story telling**. Ask for comments, observations, learnings.
    - How were they influenced?
    - How were they inspired?
    
    Facilitate a discussion as time allows.

- ☐ Be sure to **encourage all learners to continue to practice** developing situational stories and filing them into their leadership tool kit, polished and ready for situational use as appropriate.

- ☐ **And now, I'll finish the story about Terry and Cody.** Terry was coached to <u>ask for what he wanted</u>. Because of this, he was able to move to a different position of leadership that made better use of his talents, skills and style. But he was only there a very short time because he was quickly promoted to a Vice President position within the company, and is still there today. This story has a happy ending.

- ☐ Cody was not coached, but this situation could have been less difficult and stressful for Terry if Cody had known Terry better by building and maintaining a relationship with him to bring out his best and insure his success. A *Legacy Leader®* actively seeks to develop people to their full potential, which ultimately leads the whole organization to its desired success. While Cody often acknowledged and recognized Terry's contribution, he did not actively advocate for him, and did not provide a model of influential leadership to inspire Terry to reach his best.

# Day 2 - Afternoon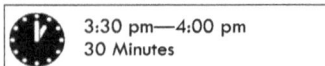

## SESSION 2-7: REFLECTIONS/WRAP/CALIBRATION

*3:30 pm—4:00 pm*
*30 Minutes*

- Volunteer Teachback
- Personal Reflections
- Community Time (Calibration)

### OBTAIN VOLUNTEER(S) FOR TEACHBACK (5 minutes)

*(Suggested times shown in parentheses after heading)*

☐ Ask for volunteer(s) to provide a 10-minute review, or teachback, of the learnings from this day. They can present in any way they like—encourage them to use their imaginations. They may use any of the materials given to them, and anything in the room. Make flip charts, etc. available. Small teams or partners can work together. Reinforce that it would be ideal if everyone had an opportunity to do this, whether alone or in partnership with others. The only thing you ask is that they ably summarize all the day's learnings in 10 minutes. There are no other guidelines!

☐ Thank the volunteer(s) from this morning again, and let the new one(s) know they will be presenting first thing the following morning. Thank them for their participation.

### PERSONAL REFLECTIONS (10 minutes)

☐ Refer participants to page 50 in the Participant Workbook. Allow them 10 minutes to reflect and capture their thoughts about what they have experienced and learned today, including Leader Partner Feedback. (Facilitator(s) may wish to write down a few of their own thoughts at this time as well, on the next page.)

### COMMUNITY TIME (15 minutes)

☐ This serves as the day-end calibration time, allows for flexibility in time scheduling, and also makes an excellent use of the Facilitator(s)' expertise. *(If you have deferred any questions that have come up during the day, this is the time to answer them.)*
  ☐ Encourage questions and answers.
  ☐ Encourage learning more about one another
  ☐ Encourage sharing experiences, outstanding learnings, etc.
  ☐ **Encourage/discuss homework (page 51 Participant Workbook)**
  ☐ Continue informal conversation until close of day

### DAY 2 CLOSE

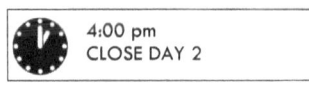

*4:00 pm*
*CLOSE DAY 2*

# Day 2 - Personal Notes — Facilitator

*Use this page to record any notes you have about your facilitation of Day 2 of the Institute*

# Day 3

# Day 3 - Overview — Morning

| SESSION | CLOCK | TIME ALLOTED | ACTIVITY | DETAILS |
|---|---|---|---|---|
| **1** INTRO (9:00-9:30) 30 min | 9:00-9:05 | 5 minutes | WELCOME | Good morning and welcome back! General welcome time. Day's plan. |
| | 9:05-9:20 | 15 minutes | TEACHBACK AND DISCUSSION | Volunteer(s) deliver(s) teachback of previous Day's learnings, with follow-up brief discussion, questions. Be quick! |
| | 9:20-9:30 | 10 minutes | DEBRIEF HOMEWORK | Ask for participants' insights, feedback regarding homework. Do not spend too much time on this. |
| **2** Best Practice #2 (9:30—10:15) 45 minutes | 9:30-9:40 | 10 minutes | BP 2—DEFINING THE TERMS EXCERCISE | Definitions exercise of all 3 terms associated with BP2—CREATOR, COLLABORATION, INNOVATION. Ask for examples of each, as object lessons. Discuss meanings, applications. (Creative approach! See Guide) |
| | 9:40-9:50 | 10 minutes | BP2—CONTENT DELIVERY | Deliver content of BP2 using Field Guide, FAC Guide, and any other materials. Share personal experiences. |
| | 9:50-10:05 | 15 minutes | BP2—AEROTECH (Review only) | Refer participants to Aerotech Briefing (Participant Workbook), as an example of a real need for collaboration on the highest and most complicated level. (Reading of these pages was assigned as homework night before.) Ask for comments, suggestions to solve Aerotech's problems. If time permits, ask for examples of their own collaboration and innovation experiences. (i.e., how does this case study compare to actual business experiences?) *(Facilitator may wish to use more creative approach to debrief these intensive pages. Remember to stay within time frame!)* |
| | 10:05-10:15 | 10 minutes | BP2—TRUST ASSESSMENT | Use assessment "Building Trust That Leads to a Team's Collaborative Innovation Competencies." (Participant Workbook) Ask participants to complete the self-assessment quickly—no double thinking (in about 3-5 minutes). Discuss as time allows. How will higher levels of trust impact your team? |
| | 10:15-10:30 | 15 minutes | BREAK | **Informal, in room or out** |
| **3** Best Practice #4 (10:30—12:00) 1 hr 30 min | 10:30-10:40 | 10 minutes | BP4—DEFINING THE TERMS EXERCISE | Definitions exercise of all 3 terms associated with BP4—ADVOCATOR, DIFFERENCES, COMMUNITY. Ask for examples of each, as object lessons. Discuss meanings, applications. *(Use different approaches to these defining exercises!)* |
| | 10:40-10:55 | 15 minutes | BP4—CONTENT DELIVERY | Deliver content of BP4 using Field Guide, FAC Guide and other matls, personal experiences, etc. Use creative approach. BP5 may be most neglected but BP4 is most misunderstood of BPs. Not about cultural diversity, but about differences in people in general (department to department, area to area, working habits, skills, personality types, etc.). |
| | 10:55-11:10 | 15 Minutes | BP4—CASE STUDIES (Prep) | Introduce BP4 Case Studies in Participant Workbook. Assign 1 to each person (or work in pairs, teams, depending on size of group—1 case study per). Allow remainder of time read, answer questions, prepare to present case and their findings. |
| | 11:10-11:30 | 20 minutes | BP4—CASE STUDIES PRESENTATIONS | Have participants read the case study and present their findings. Facilitate any discussion. These should be debriefed quickly if possible. Be sure BP4 key points are highlighted during discussion. |
| | 11:30-12:00 | 30 minutes | PCSI (or other tool) | Introduce participants to the PCSI, or other styles tool (Facilitator's choice). Explain concepts, how this can be used to determine the strengths of others. |
| | 12:00-1:00 | 1 hour | LUNCH | **In or out (depending on facility)** |

Day 3 continued next page... *(AFTERNOON)*

# Day 3 - Overview — Afternoon

| SESSION | CLOCK | TIME ALLOTED | ACTIVITY | DETAILS |
|---|---|---|---|---|
| **4** Analysis and Planning (1:00—2:20) 1 hr 20 min | 1:00-1:20 | 20 minutes | LLCI, Part 2 ANALYSIS OF OTHER'S LLCI | Participants will be coaching each other (partners). Refer them to the Participant Workbook and walk them through. Allow them remainder of this time to complete their analysis, and prepare for coaching after lunch. |
| | 1:20-1:50 | 30 minutes | LLCI—COACHING ONE ANOTHER | Allow participants to coach each other around their analysis of the other's LLCI, 15 minutes each. Hold firm to this time, and call for the switch. If not doing "pairs," may need to orchestrate the switch. |
| | 1:50-2:20 | 30 minutes | DEVELOPMENT PLANNING | Refer participants to Development Planning pages in Participant Workbook. Explain purpose. Give 30 minutes of quiet time to answer the questions there. If they need personal help, circulate to discuss. It is a good idea to have participants as separate as possible so they have private |
| | 2:20-2:35 | 15 minutes | BREAK | Informal, in or out |
| **5** Summaries (2:35—3:30) 55 min | 2:35-2:50 | 15 minutes | KNOW-BELIEVE-DO SUMMARY | Revisit the charts made on first day of what a leader must know, believe and do. Ask for any additions, revisions, etc. Refer to the "Know-Believe-Do" summary for Legacy Leaders in the Participant Workbook. Discuss all 5 BPs. |
| | 2:50-3:00 | 10 minutes | LL OVERVIEW EXERCISE— BUILDING THE HOUSE OF LEGACY LEADERSHIP (Prep) | Participants determine the relationship of the BPs to each other. A worksheet in the journal has 5 blocks that form the shape of a house. They must independently determine which block represents which BP, jotting down their comments in bullet point fashion to share with others. They are to determine why certain parts were chosen to represent certain BPs, and how the 5 relate to each other. Allow 10 minutes |
| | 3:00-3:15 | 15 minutes | LL OVERVIEW (Participant sharing) | Have each person show their Legacy "house" and explain their thoughts. Take turns and make comments as appropriate. See how people differ in their interpretation of the interrelationship of the 5 BPs. Discuss. |
| | 3:15-3:30 | 15 minutes | REVIEW ORIGINAL OBJECTIVES | Review the objectives of this Institute given on first day as stated in Participant Workbook. Determine if objectives have been met. Discuss any questions still remaining. |
| **6** Final Close (3:30-4:30) 1 Hr. | 3:30-3:40 | 10 minutes | PERSONAL REFLECTION | Capture Day 3's key learnings, personal reflection, in Participant Workbook (can also ask each person to share one key point with others if time allows). |
| | 3:40-4:10 | 30 minutes | WRAP-UP AND COMMUNITY TIME | Time for questions and answers, learning more about each other, questioning of experts, sharing experiences, outstanding learnings, etc. Applaud the efforts of the participants. Award certificates. |
| | 4:10-4:30 | 20 minutes | CELEBRATION AND ACKNOWLEDGEMENT | Time to award certificates, acknowledge participants' work and participation. Discuss follow-up to Institute (Legacy Community, products, etc.) |
| | 4:30 | | CLOSE DAY 3 | **Thank everyone for a great Institute!** |

*PLEASE NOTE DAY 3's LATER CLOSE TIME—4:30!!*

*Day 3 Summary next page...*

# Day 3 - Overview — Summary

**Day 3 SUMMARY**

**Morning**
| | | |
|---|---|---|
| Session 3-1 | Intro | 30 minutes |
| Session 3-2 | Best Practice #2 | 45 minutes |

*Morning break*

| | | |
|---|---|---|
| Session 3-3 | Best Practice #4/PCSI | 1 hour 30 minutes |

*Lunch break*

**Afternoon**
| | | |
|---|---|---|
| Session 3-4 | Analysis and Planning | 1 hour 20 minutes |

*Afternoon break*

| | | |
|---|---|---|
| Session 3-5 | Summaries | 55 minutes |
| Session 3-(6) | Wrap/Calibration/Awards | 1 hour |
| Close | | |

Official 3-Day Legacy Leadership® Institute is completed

# Day 3 — PREPARATION

**PREPARATION**

No additional preparation is required for the morning session. Participants need Participant Workbooks/PCSIs (or other tool, Facilitator's choice), pencils, pens, flip charts, etc.

No additional preparation is required for the afternoon session, except prepared certificates (optional) should be available.

Participants need Participant Workbooks, pencils, pens, flip charts, etc.

# Day 3 — TARGET GOALS

**GOALS FOR MORNING SESSION, DAY 3**

**Session 3-1: Intro**
- Welcome back
- Teachback and Discussion
- Debrief Homework

This is a warm-up session to begin the morning. The intention is to continue to get to know one another better, to provide for interaction in teachbacks and to quickly debrief the homework. Facilitator allows teachback and quick discussion, followed by questions regarding the homework. Last night's homework was to do one or all of: Developing Vision, Developing Values worksheets, Reviewing vision statement exercise in (translating vision statements for personal application), reviewing the Field Guide and other materials about Best Practices 1, 3, and 5, and Journal answers to questions about inspirational leadership. These exercises serve as a way to deepen the Legacy Leadership® experience, utilizing the participant's own time, rather than Institute time. This morning debrief acts only as a calibration/debrief of those times.

**Session 2-2: Best Practice #2**
- Defining the Terms Exercise
- BP2 Content Delivery
- BP2 "How To" Exercise
- BP2 Introduction to Creator of Collaboration and Innovation™

This session is designed to bring the participant to a new level of understanding in Best Practice 2—Creator of Collaboration and Innovation™. This is accomplished through defining the terms (CREATOR, COLLABORATION, INNOVATION) walking through the Field Guide definitions and distinctions in more detail, sharing personal experiences, reviewing teachpoints, and allowing participants to give some thought to how this BP is actually accomplished in the work place. A review of the Aerotech Briefing* (in Participant Workbook) is done quickly to show an example of collaboration and innovation on a large scale in a simulated corporate environment. One element of successful collaboration and innovation is TRUST, which is explored briefly through the "Building Trust That Leads to a Team's Collaborative Innovation Competencies" self-assessment. Meetings, where collaboration and innovation come together, is also discussed with practical information for their successful outcome. (*Please note the Aerotech Briefing is completely optional at Facilitator's choice. May be time dependent.)

**Session 3-3: Best Practice #4 and the PCSI**
- BP4 Defining the Terms Exercise
- BP4 Delivery of Content
- BP4 Case Studies
- PCSI (or other tool)

This session is designed to bring the participant to a new level of understanding in Best Practice 4—Advocator of Differences and Community™. This is accomplished through defining the terms (ADVOCATOR, DIFFERENCES, COMMUNITY) walking through the Field Guide definitions and distinctions in more detail, sharing personal experiences, reviewing teachpoints, and allowing participants to give some thought to how this BP is actually accomplished in the work place through actual case studies. The Personal Coaching Styles Inventory (PCSI)© developed by Drs. Smith and Sandstrom is also introduced as a tool to be used to determine the strengths of self and others, which can be very helpful in this best practice. (Facilitator may choose to use another similar tool in place of PCSI.) Some discussion is also devoted to explaining why this best practice is perhaps the least understood of all five, but one of the most important.

*Goals continued, next page...*

# Day 3 — TARGET GOALS

**GOALS FOR AFTERNOON SESSION, DAY 3**

### Session 3-4: Analysis and Planning
- LLCI, Part 2—Analysis of Partner's LLCI
- LLCI, Part 2—Coaching Partner to LLCI
- Development Planning

The analysis portion of partner's LLCI takes place immediately before lunch during the last part of the morning sessions. This is intended to give participants an opportunity to evaluate another person's responses to these self-assessment questions and to become more familiar with the foundational behaviors of Legacy Leadership®. The afternoon begins with coaching sessions between the partners, allowing them to give feedback to one another for the purpose of helping others develop their plan to become true Legacy Leaders®. Immediately after these activities, participants will spend time working on their own development plans for both personal and organization implementation of Legacy Leadership® (Mapping the Plan information can be reviewed here for organizational input.)

### Session 3-5: Summaries
- Know-Believe-Do Summary
- Review Original Objectives
- LL Overview—Building the House of Legacy

This session is designed to "wrap up" the basics of Legacy Leadership®, providing a summary of the Institute's learnings. The Know-Believe-Do will refer back to the original exercise when participants determined what a good leader knows, believes, and does, and will then compare that to the same outline for a Legacy Leader®. The "Building the House of Legacy" exercise is intended to allow participants to determine and discuss the relationships of the best practices to each other. This is also designed to allow them to "teach back" their own understanding of these practices. There is also a time provided for a review of the original objectives discussed on the first day, to determine if all personal objectives have been met, and discuss any unanswered questions.

### Session 3-6: Reflection/Wrap/Calibration
- Personal Reflection
- Community Time (Calibration time)
- Celebration

Time is allowed for participants to write their thoughts in the personal Reflections section of the Participant Workbook, and to recap Day 3's learnings (no teachback as on other days). It serves to calibrate the day's events. (The Community Time at the end of the day is also meant to allow some flexibility in timing of exercises, and to handle discussion of any ideas or questions that cannot be addressed at other times.)

NOTE: Facilitator(s) may wish to schedule in a brief "award" time at the end of the day to hand out certificates, generally congratulate participants and encourage their continued practice and learning of Legacy Leadership®, and inform of continuing opportunities to build legacy community.

# Day 3 - Morning — Session 3-1

**SESSION 3-1: INTRO**

 9:00 am—9:30 am
30 Min.

**WELCOME (5 minutes)**

- Welcome back
- Teachback and Discussion
- Debrief Homework

☐ Welcome participants back to another Day of Legacy Learning!

*(Suggested times shown in parentheses after heading)*

**TEACHBACK AND DISCUSSION (15 minutes)**

☐ **Introduce volunteer(s) doing teachback.** Give them the floor for approximately 10 minutes to teach back, in whatever method they choose, the learnings from Day 2.

☐ Facilitate a **brief discussion about the teachback** and take any remaining questions about Day 2. Keep this quick and laser like. Watch the clock!

**DEBRIEF HOMEWORK (10 minutes)**

☐ Ask participants for their insights regarding homework, which was one or all of the following:
- "Developing Vision"/"Developing Values" worksheets
- Read Aerotech Briefing (preparation for exercise today)
- Review the Field Guide and other materials about Best Practices 1, 3, and 5
- Journal answers to questions about influential leadership

Spend some time debriefing their work, asking and answering questions. This is a BRIEF time of review. Hold detailed questions to end of day. NOTE: While this is the last day of the 3-day Institute, there is also homework provided on Day 3. Remind learners that they are now students of leadership, and that their learning continues. It does not stop on this last day of the Institute. Encourage them to take advantage of all learning opportunities, including further exploring undiscussed materials in the Participant Workbook, and the suggested homework for Day 3.

# Day 3 - Morning

## Session 3-2

**SESSION 3-2: BEST PRACTICE #2**

9:30 am—10:15 am
45 Min.

- BP2—Defining the Terms
- BP2—Content Delivery
- BP2—Aerotech Review
- BP2— Trust Assessment

*(Suggested times shown in parentheses after heading)*

### DEFINING THE TERMS EXERCISE (10 minutes)

☐ Direct participants to page 54 of their Participant Workbook. Ask them to provide their own definitions of all 3 terms associated with BP2—CREATOR, COLLABORATION, INNOVATION™. Give them a few minutes to think and write, then ask for examples, object lessons, metaphors, etc. Discuss meanings, understandings, applications to BP2. (Remember, use the CREATIVE approach!)

### BP 2 CONTENT DELIVERY (10 minutes)

☐ This may be accomplished at the Facilitator(s)' discretion. Facilitator should be fully prepared in advance by reading the section of the Field Guide that pertains to BP2 (Participant Workbook pp 171-180). It is suggested that content refer to the Model frequently. If desired, take participants to the Field Guide for quick content review.

☐ It may not be feasible or even desirable to completely read through all the material presented in the Field Guide, or any other materials. Be sure participants are familiar with it, however, and encourage them to review in depth on their own.

☐ This should be an informal discussion, not necessarily a "lecture" format. Be sure to impart the basics of this best practice, including the teachpoints. (These are an elaboration of the points found on the Model.)

☐ As an example of the workplace application of this best practice, introduce the concept of BP2 in meetings. Begin this by saying that these are comments we hear all the time:
- I wish we could have meetings that actually accomplished something
- Our group is so divided. It's always an "us" against "them."

☐ Go on to say that you enjoy addressing these comments, because Legacy Leadership® has an answer, but begin by asking the question: "Whose job is it to ensure that meetings are productive?" Discuss answers.

**NOTE:** The Facilitator may choose to open BP2 with this kind of discussion first, even before the delivery of content. The issue of meetings is a common denominator in every corporate environment. Remember, however, that this is a 10-minute total delivery time!

# Day 3 - Morning — Session 3-2

**SESSION 3-2: BEST PRACTICE #2 (continued)**

**BP 2 CONTENT DELIVERY (continued)**

## BP2 Main Teach Points

(Found on back of LL Model)

1. **Be creative and foster trusting environment**—Building trust is the critical first step to creating a climate where innovation and collaboration can be allowed, encouraged and eventually flourish.

2. **Masterfully listen and facilitate**—Legacy Leaders® don't take control of meetings, force their own opinions on their teams or monopolize the floor – by facilitating discussions - using open-ended questions, drawing out the views and opinions of others and choosing to be still and listen – boundaries can expand to create a collaborative, innovative workplace.

3. **Acknowledge the unknown and think beyond it**—We all work within rules, processes and guidelines. Acknowledge they exist while stretching others to go "outside the box"... if this problem was 100X worse – how could we solve this problem with creativity and breakthrough thinking?

4. **Gather perspectives and ask tough question**—Be known as a leader who is open to multiple, diverse and even opposite positions in the interest of making the best decision with the best thinking supporting it.

5. **Discern need for change and project the innovative impact**—Legacy Leaders® draw out the compelling business reasons for change, get buy-in from the team and paint a positive picture of the future; the future that is full of the excitement of innovative solutions.

☐ Lead into a discussion around these issues:
- The Legacy Leader® as facilitator, CREATOR of BP2 in meetings
- How can the leader create trust in a group?
- Learn a process that always gets results (accomplishments)
- Identify what needs to be different
- How to drastically improve the environment of your meetings and turn them into collaborative sessions with highly successful outcomes
- Allow ample time and provision for disagreements and agreements
- How can all this happen?

# Day 3 - Morning — Session 3-2

**SESSION 3-2: BEST PRACTICE #2 (continued)**

### BP 2—REVIEW OF AEROTECH BRIEFING (15 minutes)

- ☐ Refer participants to pages 130-139 of the Participant Workbook. This was assigned as homework, so hopefully they have read it already. Explain this is an example of a need for collaboration in a highly complex case. Walk them through the first 3 introductory pages <u>quickly</u>.

- ☐ Next show learners the individual team instructions and background sheets for the individual departments within Aerotech. *(point out highlights, do not read!)*

- ☐ Discuss the needs for collaboration and innovation and how that might have been utilized for a project of this scope. Discuss relationship of this briefing to actual work experiences the learners may have had. *(NOTE: The Facilitator may choose to present and discuss this exercise in any manner they choose. The purpose is to allow a small group to see a large exercise, and the need for creation of collaboration and innovation on a large corporate scale. TRY not to spend more than allotted time on this briefing review.)*

### BP2 TRUST ASSESSMENT (10 Minutes)

- ☐ Refer learners to page 56 in their Participant Workbooks. Introduce and walk-through this assessment "Building Trust That Leads to a Team's Collaborative Innovation Competencies" quickly.

- ☐ Ask participants to complete the self-assessment quickly—no double thinking (in about 3-5 minutes).

- ☐ Discuss as time allows. *(NOTE: It is possible that time will not be available for this exercise. If this is the case, encourage them to complete the trust assessment on their own, highlighting the importance of establishing trust within a collaborative environment. This will be part of their ongoing learning as students of leadership.)*

**MORNING BREAK (15 minutes)**

> 10:15 am—10:30 am
> BREAK 15 minutes

# Day 3 - Morning     Session 3-3

**SESSION 3-3: BEST PRACTICE #4**

10:30 am—11:40 am
1 Hour 10 minutes

- BP4—Defining the Terms
- BP4—Content Delivery
- BP4—Case Studies
- PCSI (or other tool)

**DEFINING THE TERMS EXERCISE (10 minutes)**

*(Suggested times shown in parentheses after heading)*

☐ Once again, use the creative approach to this defining exercise. Direct participants to page 59 of their Participant Workbook. Provide definitions of all 3 terms associated with BP4—ADVOCATOR, DIFFERENCES, COMMUNITY™. Ask for examples, object lessons, metaphors, etc. Discuss meanings, understandings, applications to BP4.

**BP 4 CONTENT DELIVERY (15 minutes)**

**Facilitator Note:** BP4 may be introduced by actually telling or reading the first case study (page 66 Participant Workbook) to illustrate the often misunderstood meaning of this BP.

☐ This may be accomplished at the Facilitator(s)' discretion. Facilitator should be fully prepared in advance by reading the section of the Field Guide that pertains to BP4 (pp 181-190). It is suggested that content refer to the Model frequently. If desired, take participants to the Field Guide for <u>quick</u> content review. Use Aerial Views!

☐ It may not be feasible or even desirable to completely read through all the material presented in the Field Guide, or any other materials. Be sure participants are familiar with it, however, and encourage them to review in depth on their own.

☐ This should be an **informal discussion**, not necessarily a "lecture" format (but a lecture format can be used for delivering content just as easily—this is Facilitator's choice). Be sure to impart the basics of this best practice, including the teachpoints on next page. *(These are an elaboration of the points found on the back of the Model.)*

☐ *It is extremely important to highlight the fact that this **Best Practice is NOT about cultural diversity**, as many might think. This is often misunderstood. This is about making a community of diverse parts, individuals who vary by background, training, education, skills, habits, personalities, departments, genders, etc., etc., etc. It is about celebrating the differences and advocating for the whole created by them. Make sure this point is understood!*

# Day 3 - Morning — Session 3-3

**SESSION 3-3: BEST PRACTICE #4 (continued)**

## BP4 Main Teach Points

(Found on back of LL Model)

1. **Be an advocate for people and raise their visibility**—The leader moves beyond the traditional definitions of diversity, but is an advocate for all constituents, regardless of age, experience, seniority, status, etc.

2. **Recognize strengths and build value**—A Legacy Leader® knows that each individual has unique strengths. All of these strengths are recognized and encouraged to build value for the entire team or organization.

3. **Build diverse teams**—By actively seeking to build strength through differences, the Legacy Leader acts with intention in creating strong teams, filled with delightful opposites and uniquenesses for a united and complete team.

4. **Promote an inclusive environment**—Everyone brings something and is welcomed – we look beyond the surface and accept what may seem strange or unusual culturally, socially, style-wise or otherwise.

5. **Recognize impact of business directions and communicate appropriately**—The Legacy Leader® must be aware of how his or her leadership or organizational direction impacts others internally and externally. The entire community must be kept informed of these directions.

### BP4—CASE STUDIES (Preparation) (15 Minutes)

- Refer participants to pages 66-71 of the Participant Workbook. Explain that these are **case studies of typical** (some actual) situations in which a real understanding and application of Best Practice 4 is needed.

- **Assign one case study to each participant** (or have them work in pairs/groups, each team assigned one case study, depending on total number of participants). Give them the remaining time of this segment (15 minutes) to read over the case study, and answer the questions presented with each. They will report back to the group when the time is completed for preparation. Direct them to page 65 in their Participant Workbooks to take notes during this preparation.

**Facilitator Note:** Watch the time on this exercise and discussion! Allow at least 10 minutes at end of this session for styles inventory discussion. This has been very helpful for Institute participants in understanding BP4.

### BP4—CASE STUDIES (Presentation) (20 Minutes)

- Ask participants to **read their assigned case study and the questions, then their responses** to the questions. Debrief and discuss as necessary. *(The next several pages in this guide present the suggested responses.)* Watch the time!

- **Point out page 64** in the Participant Workbook. This page contains questions they can ask themselves and their business teams to have a better understanding of how to apply this BP4.

# Day 3 - Morning — Session 3-3

**SESSION 3-3: BEST PRACTICE #4 (continued)**

**BP4—CASE STUDIES (Debrief Information, Suggested Responses)**

☐ **Case Study 1**

**What is the real issue (or issues) they face?**
There is a big hole in the team. Where is the operations person who will make sure the product gets out the door, whose strength it is to handle customers and keep them happy?

**Strengths:**
- Jim, President: A take charge, bottom-line visionary, loves new projects, background product development.
- Bill, Marketing/Sales VP: Charismatic guy, persuasive, high level ethics. Doesn't like to deliver, just sell.
- Greg, Product Developer: loves to build new products, likes new projects all the time. But might not be good at delivery of product
- Mary, Financial VP: persuasive and outgoing, works well with venture capitalists. Doing well managing the financial side of the business.
- MISSING IN ACTION: An operations person who is really good at handling the project orientation and logistics of product delivery.

**The consultant will say,** "Get the product delivered, and get the customers happy or there will be no more investment."

**What would a Legacy Leader® do in this case?**
A Legacy Leader® would from the very beginning analyze the basic strengths needed for each business area and make sure the right people were in the right positions. LLs are also connoisseurs of talent, making sure that individuals are working from their strengths and experience areas, and that the team is complete with all necessary talent.

☐ **Case Study 2**

**Real issue:**
The team has not accepted responsibility for giving their undivided attention to each person on the team. Because Fuji's language is difficult to understand, they allow their minds to wander, and like a lot of team members, begin to take care of their own concerns rather than be invested in listening to input that could make a big difference in the team's success. The challenge for Roberto is making sure that Fuji's ideas area heard and that the team understands thoroughly.

**Why is the rest of the group not listening?**
Since Fuji is new to the group, it is possible that he is not known very well by the team. Also, Roberto has not set the stage or environment for members to give their full attention to each other, learning from each other, and developing synergistically. So, their attentions wander when they grow impatient with someone who is taking a long time to express himself.

# Day 3 - Morning  Session 3-3

**SESSION 3-3: BEST PRACTICE #4 (continued)**

**BP4—CASE STUDIES (Debrief Information, Suggested Responses) (continued)**

☐ **Case Study 2 (continued)**

**What should Roberto do?**
He should immediately call the group's attention to the pattern that is beginning to be established in the group; i.e. that every time Fuji speaks, people stop listening. He should share that Fuji's ideas and input are critical to the team. He might also ask if someone else (besides himself) could paraphrase what they just heard Fuji say. If no one can do so, then Fuji would be given another chance to contribute his ideas as the whole team listens, asks questions for full understanding of Fuji, helps him be heard, and all learn from the input, thereby establishing a better group pattern. Roberto can turn help the team turn this around. If the leader does not, then some informal leader could also bring this to the attention of the group.

**What would a Legacy Leader® do to make this a learning possibility?**
The LL creates an environment of respect for all group members, valuing their opinions and expecting everyone to do the same. Each person is specifically chosen for his/her diverse opinions and contributions. The better the leader models listening, learning and understanding, the more likely the group members will as well.

☐ **Case Study 3**

**What should Chris ask for from Jake?**
She should state that her strengths are not being utilized and that her hands are tied in the group.

If she wants to stay, she might ask Jake to intervene in the environment of the team by leading the way to make sure everyone hears her ideas, that they are respected and implemented. She might also ask for his help in her intervention in the team.

If she wants to resign, she should ask for what she wants, (recommendation, severance, etc.) If she can't decide what she wants, she should ask Jake for help in deciding by asking what his real motive was for hiring her and how that is working for him.

**What are her prospects with the team, and can she herself do anything about it?**
At this point her prospects are not good since there has not been a leader who would set the stage for full participation by everyone. She could also ask for that from the leader.

**What should Jake do when confronted with this?**
Hopefully, Jake can realize that he is missing a great opportunity by having a team that doesn't pay attention (nor does he) to a valuable player, one that can make a great impact on the team, and the community of customers.

## Day 3 - Morning — Session 3-3

**SESSION 3-3: BEST PRACTICE #4 (continued)**

**BP4—CASE STUDIES (Debrief Information, Suggested Responses) (continued)**

☐ **Case Study 3 (continued)**

**What would a Legacy Leader® to in this situation?**
As a Legacy Leader®, Jake would create an environment where everyone's strengths are utilized, where everyone's perspectives are heard, and where together the team is successful because of all the unique talents of the whole.

Chris as a Legacy Leader® would state her vision of how the company is represented to the community, about how the company can be distinct from its competitors as well as inclusive of the community members.

**Where do these events leave the community?**
It is left with a corporate citizen that appears to be more internally focused (exclusive) than externally focused (inclusive), who appears to be stuck in old ways of doing things and missing new opportunities that workers could take advantage of.

☐ **Case Study 4**

**Does this company need to bend to the news report and do something different? If so, why?**
If they do nothing, the company will have major fallout in the press and in their competitive markets. Their stock prices could plummet unless handled carefully. Global markets would not want to be involved unless local community leadership could occur. So, yes, something needs to be done. At the very least they must state the policy of the merged company about how to handle such placements.

**If you were the new President coming in to lead the company, what would you do about this situation?**
As a Legacy Leader®, I would immediately establish the direction and values associated with placement of leaders around the world, not just in these particular areas. I would be an advocate for all people, recognize their strengths and build value, build diverse teams, and promote an inclusive environment. By doing so, I would be recognizing the impact of business direction and communicate it appropriately.

**What strengths and attributes should be considered for the leaders of these remote sites?**
On a location by location basis, each leadership position should be evaluated for what is most needed there. Of great value would be those individuals who had the experience and the knowledge of the networks in the community that would be to the company's advantage. The leader could also assign a mentor who would bridge the gap between the local community and the leadership team.

## SESSION 3-3: BEST PRACTICE #4 (continued)

### BP4—CASE STUDIES (Debrief Information, Suggested Responses) (continued)

☐ **Case Study 5**

**What does George need most right now?**
George must begin to understand that he has much to gain by fully developing his people. If he wants the best for them, the best is to be fully developed for the upcoming business needs. Just as they have followed his lead for a long time, he can help them see that it is in their best interest to be prepared for the future. It would be a great disservice to them and the company not to utilize and develop their full potential.

**How can he do what is asked of him and ensure the trust he has always had with his employees?**
George will need to be clear with his boss what her full intentions are. He could express his concerns that some people are being set up to be let go. Once assured of her real intentions, he can begin to create the environment for gathering the data she has requested. He will need to frame the requests in a way that could provide some realistic hope for their development, and whether they stay or leave the company.

**Is there a way for him to be positive about this situation?**
When George begins to see that it is riskier for his people to remain in status quo and not prepare them for what is to come in the future, then he will be able to be more positive. He needs to do the same for himself (determine his own strengths and the attributes needed for his current and/or future position.

**What does George's boss need to do for him?**
The boss needs to gather data about George, asking about strengths, high performance patterns, what he likes to do best, what he wants to do next, how he can contribute, what his style of learning and communication, etc. Most of all she needs to help him have a renewed commitment for developing fully the talent in his department.

**If George's boss were a Legacy Leader®**
She would be doing those things above as well as helping him establish the direction and guiding principles for his group. She would make sure he knows how to create a collaborative environment of trust, influence others to be the best they can be, hold them accountable, and help them know how important they all are to the entire organization.

# Day 3 - Morning — Session 3-3

**SESSION 3-3: BEST PRACTICE #4 (continued)**

**BP4—CASE STUDIES (Debrief Information, Suggested Responses) (continued)**

☐ **Case Study 6**

**What should Terry communicate to his boss?**
He should ask for what he wants, the kind of position, the environment (one that includes people around him). He should also let him know how unhappy he is with the current situation to see if there is anything that can be done to make it better. Also, he should let him know what potential positions within the company interest him most—then ask for the development and advocacy that will lead to a more highly contributive worker.

**What should Cody be doing to retain strong talent?**
Cody should get to know his people better, determine what environment works best, and never assume that just because a person is trained in a particular job set that he or she wants to stay there forever. If a person is highly valued within an organization, it does not work to keep them in a box, not allowing them to have a career path.

**If Legacy Leaderhip® was available, what would each be doing?**
Cody would be strongly attuned to the value and strengths that each person brings to the department. He would be an advocate for them, having them be visible to his peers, encouraging them to grow in various areas, mentoring and coaching them to be their best. He would not do this for just one favorite individual, but for all of them, regardless of how many. Such an approach needs to be a part of the culture.

*(end of case studies)*

## PERSONAL COACHING STYLES INVENTORY (PCSI)
**(30 minutes)** *or other tool (see note)*

☐ Introduce participants to the **PCSI** (separate cover). Quickly explain the background and purpose for this tool, and its relevance to this BP.

☐ Direct them to page 62 in their Participant Workbooks. Quickly go over the questions and statements there, and allow the participants **time to complete the PCSI for themselves.** (If time does not allow a complete exploration of this tool, the homework for this day will make reference to this piece.)

☐ If possible, discuss the questions presented in the Participant Workbook.

**Facilitator Note:** You may wish to use another styles inventory assessment which can be quickly taken and debriefed in this amount of time. This exercise has been helpful to participants. If you choose to use the PCSI, they are available through CoachWorks®. If you choose another tool, you can substitute the page in the Participant Workbook for one that reflects your chosen tool.

**LUNCH BREAK (1 hour)**

12:00 pm—1:00 pm
LUNCH 1 Hour

# Day 3 - Afternoon — Session 3-4

**SESSION 3-4: ANALYSIS AND PLANNING**

🕐 1:00 pm—2:20 pm
1 Hour 20 minutes

**LLCI, PART 2—ANALYSIS OF OTHER'S LLCI (20 minutes)**

- LLCI Part 2—Partner analysis
- LLCI Part 2—Partner Coaching
- Development Planning

*(Suggested times shown in parentheses after heading)*

☐ Tell participants that this is the second part of the LLCI. At this time they will be **trading LLCIs with their Leader Partner** (or other assigned person, depending on dynamics of the Institute group). **Remind learners to put their names on LLCIs.**

☐ Direct them to pages 73-75 of the Participant Workbook. Give them the rest of this allotted time to **analyze their partner's LLCI** according to the information provided in the Participant Workbook. Tell them also to utilize information from their **Leader Partner Feedback Sheet**, to illustrate or highlight any of their analysis/coaching points.

**LLCI, PART 2—COACHING ONE ANOTHER (30 minutes)**

☐ At the end of the 20 minutes, call the group's attention back, and explain that now is the **time for personal coaching.**

☐ Have participants **pair up with their partners.** Ask them to find corners of the room where they can have quiet conversations with one another. One partner begins by coaching the other for 15 minutes, using the comments and observations they made on the analysis sheets, and on their Leader Partner Feedback sheet, before lunch. **Signal the time to switch**, and allow remaining partner to be coached. Facilitator may need to keep this process on task and on time.

☐ Ask learners to **take notes and record their partner's observations** so that they may make use of this information during the following development planning session.

☐ NOTE: **Be sure to allow the full time to this exercise.** Previous Institutes have revealed that this time allows rich internalization of the Legacy Leadership® principles, and allows participants to realize they can coach others in leadership.

# Day 3 - Afternoon — Session 3-4

**SESSION 3-4: ANALYSIS AND PLANNING (continued)**

**DEVELOPMENT PLANNING (30 minutes)**

- ☐ This is the participant's **opportunity to pull it all together.** Refer them to the **Development Plan** in the Participant Workbook (pages 77-82). Here is where you take all of your learnings and make commitments to yourself to:
  - Grow and model your own skills as a Legacy Leader®
  - Describe your plan to grow other Legacy Leaders®.

- ☐ This is also a good time to reinforce that as a leader, **you get more out of building on your strengths than working through a huge list of development needs.**

- ☐ Inputs that are available to learners: *(optional – write on flip chart)*
  - Legacy Leadership® Competency Inventory results
  - Team Teach Reviews
  - Leader Partner Feedback
  - Insights gained from networking
  - Your Reflections
  - Your past experiences, skills and self-knowledge

- ☐ Ask learners to find a quiet place to do their planning. Instruct them that they have approximately **25-30 minutes to complete this exercise.** This is a **quiet time** for personal planning. The Facilitator will be available "standing by" if there are individual questions or a need for personal assistance. Focus is on quiet planning and serious preparation for real Legacy Leadership® beyond this Institute.

- ☐ **Optional:** If they finish early, ask them to find another LL who has also completed his or her plan, and **spend some time coaching each other** on the reasonableness and "doability" of his or her Development Plan, including ensuring that their commitments to self are challenging and achievable. Every opportunity they have to network and to insert accountability into this process will help them reach their goals.

**MAPPING THE PLAN (repeat, optional)**

- ☐ Depending on time, Facilitator may also choose to **review again the "Mapping the Plan" exercise** on page 213 of the Participant Workbook (also p. 38 Participant Workbook). This form, in addition to providing excellent feedback and accountability for Best Practice #5, serves as a good way to plan for organizational development as well, and is a good complement to the personal development plan.

**AFTERNOON BREAK (15 minutes)**

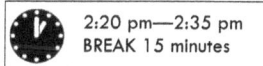
2:20 pm—2:35 pm
BREAK 15 minutes

# Day 3 - Afternoon Session 3-5

**SESSION 3-5: SUMMARIES**

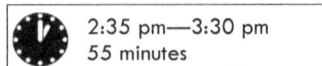
2:35 pm—3:30 pm
55 minutes

**KNOW-BELIEVE-DO SUMMARY (15 minutes)**

- Know-Believe-Do Summary
- LL Overview Exercise—Building the House of Legacy
- Review Original Objectives

*(Suggested times shown in parentheses after heading)*

☐ **Refer learners back to the chart** you constructed on the first day when identifying the "ideal leader." This is the chart divided in columns with the headings "What does the ideal leader: **KNOW, BELIEVE, DO.**"

☐ Next, refer participants to page 83 in the Participant Workbook, which is the Legacy Leadership® summary of the same items—What a LEGACY LEADER® MUST KNOW, BELIEVE AND DO.

☐ Take about 15 minutes to **compare the two charts** and see if the items mentioned the first day are covered on the Legacy Leadership® version. Discuss and debrief as needed. Indicate that Legacy Leadership® embraces every aspect of excellent leadership practices.

**LEGACY LEADERSHIP OVERVIEW—THE HOUSE OF LEGACY (Preparation) (10 minutes)**

☐ The basic intent of this is to get learners to think about and discuss their personal ideas of how Legacy Leadership® works, and specifically **how the 5 Best Practices interrelate.**

☐ Refer participants to page 84 in the Participant Workbook. There is a picture of 5 shapes that together make a house. This is the **"House of Legacy."** Ask the learners to give some thought to the **interrelationships** of the five best practices. Have them assign one BP to each of the shapes. Each participant may see these interrelationships in different terms. For example, one may see the roof as BP1, another as BP3, etc. Give them the remainder of these 10 minutes to make their determinations and notes on the sheet supporting their choices. Tell them to be prepared to share their "houses" and their logic behind them as a summary review of what they have learned about Legacy Leadership®. Ask them also to consider the element of balance as the five best practices relate to one another.

☐ After the preparation time is complete, ask for **volunteers to share their thoughts about the House of Legacy.** Continue until each who wishes has shared their thoughts. Discuss differences seen between participants and facilitate an overall summary discussion about the relationships of the 5 Best Practices to each other. How does the issue of balance apply here?

# Day 3 - Afternoon — Session 3-5

**SESSION 3-5: SUMMARIES (continued)**

**REVIEW ORIGINAL OBJECTIVES (15 minutes)**

- ☐ **Refer back to the original objectives from Day 1** (posted on the wall). Now that we are almost finished with the formal LL Institute, we want to ensure that all original objectives were met. Not only the objectives of this Institute, but hopefully your personal objectives as well. If not, we want to have a solution before you leave!

- ☐ As a group, look at the objectives (page 16 of the Participant Workbook) one by one and ask **"Was this objective met in the Institute? How?"** Discuss.

- ☐ As time allows, have each learner go back to their **personal objective** for the Institute (on their partner introduction sheet, page 14 in Participant Workbook). Ask the same questions. If any objectives are still unmet, discuss any further opportunities that may meet these needs. *(Facilitator(s) may determine that personal time with individuals may be necessary to discuss and give suggestions for fulfilling any still unmet objectives.)*

# Day 3 - Afternoon — Session 3-6

**SESSION 3-6: REFLECTIONS/WRAP/CALIBRATION**

3:30 pm—4:30 pm
55 minutes

- Personal Reflections
- Community Time (Calibration)
- Awards and Celebration!

*(Suggested times shown in parentheses after heading)*

**PERSONAL REFLECTIONS (10 minutes)**

☐ Refer participants to page 126 in the Participant Workbook. Allow them 10 minutes to reflect and capture their thoughts about what they have experienced and learned in the day. *(Facilitator(s) may wish to write down a few of their own thoughts at this time as well, on the next pages.)*

**COMMUNITY TIME (30 minutes or time remaining)**

☐ This serves as the day-end calibration time, allows for flexibility in time scheduling, and also makes an excellent use of the Facilitator(s)' expertise. *(If you have deferred any questions that have come up during the day, this is the time to answer them.)* Use this time also to teachback Day 3's learnings in creative ways.

**CELEBRATION AND ACKNOWLEDGEMENT (20 minutes or time remaining)**

☐ Facilitator(s) may need to plan ahead for allowing some time for final activities, including the awarding of certificates (optional) or any other finalizing events or details to wrap up the Institute. Celebrate the group and individual achievements by acknowledging each person.

☐ Spend a few moments to tell learners that the **adventure continues.** They are students of leadership and the learning is never done. Remind of Day 3 homework opportunity, the "More…" section of the Participant Workbook and additional resources found there, products available through CoachWorks®, and other appropriate encouragement to continue their learning.

☐ Celebrate!

**DAY 3 CLOSE**

4:30 pm
CLOSE DAY 3

**The 3-Day Legacy Leaderhip® Institute is now completed.**

# Day 3 - Personal Notes — Facilitator

*Use this page to record any notes you have about your facilitation of Day 3 of the Institute*

# Resources

**Facilitator Note:** The Legacy Leadership® Review is included in the Participant Workbook, and the answers are provided here as an additional tool that you may choose to use in your final debriefing of the Institute, or other use with your participants. This "test" is intentionally designed to get learners into the rich content of the Field Guide, which really cannot be completely covered during the Institute. If you use this tool, be sure to warn participants that they cannot simply zip off an answer. They will need to research the Field Guide for the correct answer to any of these questions. It is not a test of knowledge, but rather a tool to encourage use of Field Guide. Facilitator may choose to use this Review in any way they wish. It could even be assigned as additional homework as an extra option.

# Legacy Leadership® Review — Answers

NOTE: The Legacy Leadership® Review is specifically designed to get you into the rich content found in the Field Guide. Careful with your answers!

**Participant Name:** _____  **Date:** _____

1. **Fill in the blanks to complete the *5 Best Practices:*** 
   a. Advocator of __*Differences*__ and Community
   b. __*Holder*__ of Vision and Values
   c. Influencer of Inspiration and __*Leadership*__
   d. __*Creator*__ of Collaboration and __*Innovation*__
   e. Calibrator of __*Responsibility*__ and Accountability

2. **Which of the following *Readiness Indicators* demonstrate that a *Professional* is a prime candidate for Legacy Leadership®?**
   - _X_ I would like to inspire others, and be inspired myself, to see and reach the greatest potentials.
   - _X_ I would like my work to be fun, and also promote that environment for others.
   - ___ I would like to grow my skills to advance my career options.
   - _X_ I am ready to change my attitudes and break out of old habits to create new successes.
   - _X_ I would like to become more of a mentor, modeling leadership practices and attitudes to others in my team.
   - ___ All of the above.

3. **Which of the following are *three Behaviors and Competencies* that distinguish a *Holder of Values*:**
   - _X_ Models authenticity. Personal and professional life is seamless.
   - ___ Actively seeks to lift up others, even those "outside" immediate corporate or departmental lines.
   - _X_ Encourages others to develop, define and live personal values.
   - ___ Is self-inspired, and knows what inspires others.
   - ___ Respects others.
   - _X_ "Walks the talk" of personal core values.

4. **A Legacy Leader® who is a *Creator of Collaboration* believes in spontaneous or impromptu brainstorming sessions, which are freeform, open-ended and completely unstructured.**
   _____ True   __*X*__ False

5. **What is the *definition of a LegacyShift*™? Give one example.**
   *(A shift from one behavior to another, true to the LL model. The Legacy Leader creates the environment that generates these shifts. Example, from suspicion to trust, or from ordinary to extraordinary, etc.)*

6. **Which of the following is NOT an element of a good *Story*:**
   - ___ explanation of state of affairs
   - ___ an outcome
   - _X_ both a hero and a heroine
   - ___ setting of characters
   - ___ none of the above

# Legacy Leadership® Review — Answers

7. **Which *Best Practice* is categorized with these *Challenges or Potential Barriers*:**
   - Leaders that do not fulfill their own responsibilities
   - Lack of compassion and caring for people
   - No roadmap
   - Forgetting the customer

   ___ BP#1 – Holder of Vision and Values™
   ___ BP#2 – Creator of Collaboration and Innovation™
   ___ BP#3 – Influencer of Inspiration and Leadership™
   ___ BP#4 – Advocator of Differences and Community™
   _X_ BP#5 – Calibrator of Responsibility and Accountability™

8. **Please complete the following *definitions*:**

   ### Inspiration
   Inspiration is the process of: *Animating, motivating or encouraging others to reach new levels of achievement.*

   ### Leadership
   Leadership is the process of: *Guiding and directing others to shared success.*

   Which Best Practice embodies Inspiration and Leadership? (circle one)   1   2   **(3)**   4   5

9. **The following *Language Questions* are critical to Best Practice 5 – Calibrator of Responsibility and Accountability:** _X_ True   ___ False:
   - Questions that encourage all individual parts of "community" to contribute their very best to the process.
   - Questions that seek to determine if actions measure up to standards and levels of excellence.

10. **Provide one *Legacy Step* for each Best Practice** (one that particularly resonates with you personally):

    BP#1 – *Bring whole self to your leadership*

    BP#2 – *Do not judge ideas until all innovative thinking is on the table*

    BP#3 – *Develop an attitude of inspiration*

    BP#4 – *Become an active and eager listener.*

    BP#5 – *Encourage frequent and clear communication among all parts of the whole*

11. **How would you advise another *Legacy Leader®* to embrace the concept of *Reflection* and journaling?**

    *Set aside time each day (or at the end of a project or planning session) to capture key "Aha's," possible actions and who else could benefit from this knowledge. Is also useful to refer back to later.*

# Legacy Leadership® Review — Answers

**12. Which of the following Legacy Leadership® statements are true?** *(Check all that apply.)*
- _X_ it's about individuals, the heart of relationships
- _X_ it's about distinction and inclusion
- _X_ it's about direction and commitment
- ___ it's about doing what's best for people, no matter what
- _X_ it's about the environment of working relations
- _X_ it's about execution and performance
- ___ none of the above
- ___ all of the above

**13. Match the following *Expected Outcomes* to the associated Best Practice:**

- _3_ a. stretches to be the best
- _1_ b. has meaning and purpose for efforts
- _2_ c. puts ego aside to hear brilliance of others
- _5_ d. loyal customers
- _4_ e. reputation attractive to employees

1. Holder
2. Creator
3. Influencer
4. Advocator
5. Calibrator

**14. *An Advocator of Differences ...***
- _X_ seeks to discover how others see the world and individual situations **OR**
- ___ always has the success of the whole organization in mind

**15. *An Advocator of Community ...***
- _X_ sees beyond the boundaries of individuals, teams or departments **OR**
- ___ helps ensure that the right people are in the right positions within the organization

**16. Name 3 Resources to demonstrate the business impact of Legacy Leadership® on the bottom line *(Business Applications for Legacy Leadership®)*:** *(any referenced in LG)*

**17. How can the *LLCI* assist you to grow other leaders?** *(Check all that apply):*
- ___ tool to determine the business issues of other leaders
- ___ assessment of a great leader
- _X_ 360 view of a leader's strengths and weaknesses
- _X_ to benchmark their level of competency in each of the 5 Best Practice contexts
- ___ pass/fail of a leader's key competencies

**18. Name one *Essence Statement* for each Best Practice:**

BP#1 – *Leaders embody, hold out for all to know, company's vision and values*

BP#2 – *Leaders supply environments where team members are comfortable enough to create possibilities...*

BP#3 – *Leaders are "trailblazers" with a positive influence so that everyone is lifted up to be the best they can be*

BP#4 – *Leaders possess a mindset that all people have unique and compelling contributions to make.*

BP#5 – *Leaders who demonstrate personal standards of behavior and accountability.*

# Legacy Leadership® Review — Answers

19. An *Influencer of Inspiration and Leadership*™ builds positive, meaningful relationships with energy, enables others to lead through positive modeling and recognizes, acknowledges and inspires others.

    _____X_____ True          _____ False

20. Which of the following *Indicators* demonstrate that an *Organization* is *ready* for Legacy Leadership®?
    - ___ The Company wants leadership that sets a clear direction.
    - ___ The Company wants a healthier bottom line.
    - ___ The Company wants to attract and retain high potential employees.
    - ___ The Company wants to increase loyalty among customers.
    - ___ The Company is willing to expand out from old boundaries and learn new patterns for success.
    - ___ The Company would like a reputation in the outside corporate world of integrity and employee value.
    - _X_ All of the above.

**Score:** _____

*This is the end of the formal Legacy Leadership® Review. If there is time remaining, you may choose to complete the remaining OPTIONAL questions to give you added insight into Legacy Leadership® and the Best Practices.*

**Optional Development Questions**

21. For each Best Practice, select *one Challenge* that you feel will be <u>easiest</u> for you to overcome to get off to a fast start:

    BP#1 – Holder of Vision and Values

    BP#2 – Creator of Collaboration and Innovation

    BP#3 – Influencer of Inspiration and Leadership

    BP#4 – Advocator of Differences and Community

    BP#5 – Calibrator of Responsibility and Accountability

22. Now select *one Challenge* that you feel may take <u>additional effort</u>, resources, time or a paradigm shift for it to be overcome.

    BP#1 – Holder of Vision and Values

    BP#2 – Creator of Collaboration and Innovation

    BP#3 – Influencer of Inspiration and Leadership

    BP#4 – Advocator of Differences and Community

    BP#5 – Calibrator of Responsibility and Accountability

www.ingramcontent.com/pod-product-compliance
Lightning Source LLC
Chambersburg PA
CBHW080349170426
43194CB00014B/2735